My Sister, My Sister

by Ray Aranha

A Samuel French Acting Edition

New York Hollywood London Toronto
SAMUELFRENCH.COM

Copyright © 1973 by Ray Aranha

ALL RIGHTS RESERVED

CAUTION: Professionals and amateurs are hereby warned that *MY SISTER, MY SISTER* is subject to a Licensing Fee. It is fully protected under the copyright laws of the United States of America, the British Commonwealth, including Canada, and all other countries of the Copyright Union. All rights, including professional, amateur, motion picture, recitation, lecturing, public reading, radio broadcasting, television and the rights of translation into foreign languages are strictly reserved. In its present form the play is dedicated to the reading public only.

The amateur live stage performance rights to *MY SISTER, MY SISTER* are controlled exclusively by Samuel French, Inc., and licensing arrangements and performance licenses must be secured well in advance of presentation. PLEASE NOTE that amateur Licensing Fees are set upon application in accordance with your producing circumstances. When applying for a licensing quotation and a performance license please give us the number of performances intended, dates of production, your seating capacity and admission fee. Licensing Fees are payable one week before the opening performance of the play to Samuel French, Inc., at 45 W. 25th Street, New York, NY 10010.

Licensing Fee of the required amount must be paid whether the play is presented for charity or gain and whether or not admission is charged.

Stock licensing fees quoted upon application to Samuel French, Inc.

For all other rights than those stipulated above, apply to: William Morris Endeavor Entertainment, 1325 Avenue of the Americas, New York, NY 10019.

Particular emphasis is laid on the question of amateur or professional readings, permission and terms for which must be secured in writing from Samuel French, Inc.

Copying from this book in whole or in part is strictly forbidden by law, and the right of performance is not transferable.

Whenever the play is produced the following notice must appear on all programs, printing and advertising for the play: "Produced by special arrangement with Samuel French, Inc."

Due authorship credit must be given on all programs, printing and advertising for the play.

No one shall commit or authorize any act or omission by which the copyright of, or the right to copyright, this play may be impaired.
No one shall make any changes in this play for the purpose of production.
Publication of this play does not imply availability for performance. Both amateurs and professionals considering a production are strongly advised in their own interests to apply to Samuel French, Inc., for written permission before starting rehearsals, advertising, or booking a theatre.
No part of this book may be reproduced, stored in a retrieval system, or transmitted in any form, by any means, now known or yet to be invented, including mechanical, electronic, photocopying, recording, videotaping, or otherwise, without the prior written permission of the publisher.

ISBN 978-0-573-61272-5   Printed in U.S.A.   #15170

"MY SISTER, MY SISTER" was first presented in September, 1973, at the Hartford Stage Company, Hartford, Connecticut. Subsequently it reopened at the Little Theatre, New York City, on April 30, 1974, wih the following cast:

SUE BELLE	*Seret Scott*
MAMA	*Barbara Montgomery*
EVELINA	*Jessie Saunders*
JESUS AND WHITE MAN	*Lowell Copeland*
EDDIE AND DADDY	*David Downing*
SPECTRE	*Frank Adu*
SPECTRE	*Trazana Beverley*
SPECTRE	*Diane Bivens*
SPECTRE	*Rosanna Carter*
SPECTRE	*Larry Pertilla*

Directed by Paul Weidner.

For my daughter, Teri

"MY SISTER, MY SISTER"

(*A Play in Two Acts*)

By

RAY ARANHA

The entire play is projected from the brain of Sue Belle. That which the audience sees and hears is that which Sue Belle sees and hears or interjects upon reality.

CHARACTERS

An actor or actress may play several roles or may play a character in different emotional periods of that character's life.

Actress #1:
   SUE BELLE: *A woman at sixteen; her age in reality.*
   SUE BELLE (Child): *Six years old.*
   SUE BELLE (Adolescent): *Twelve years old.*
   SUE BELLE/EVELINA: *An intertwining of Sue Belle's personality with that of her sister, Evelina's, at her 21-year-old stage; the two interchanging in dominance.*

Actor #2:
   EDDIE: *20 to 25 years old; Sue Belle's lover.*
   DADDY: *Middle forties; Sue Belle's father; his name is Earl.*

Actress #3:
   EVELINA (Adolescent): *Fifteen years old; Sue Belle's sister.*
   EVELINA (Adult): *Twenty-one years old.*

Actress #4:
  MAMA: *Middle forties; Sue Belle's Mama; her name is Claudine.*

Actor #5:
  JESUS: *As usually pictured.*
  MAN: *Thirties.*

Two Actors and Three Actresses:

  SPECTRES: *Men dressed in dark suits with spit-polished skulls; woman dressed in long white robes and white headdresses.*

All characters except for Actor #5 are Black.

Sue Belle's changes need not be a totally physical one. Her changes are basically emotional. She remembers scenes as they happened or as she has altered them and then steps into them relating to the dialogue and action as they unfold. Sue Belle is always locked in her 16-year-old frame and any manifestations of the six-year-old Sue Belle, or the 12-year-old Sue Belle, or the stage when she takes on the traits of her sister are initially internal ones, with any outward vocal or physical change, if any, coming as a result of the internal.

TIME AND PLACE

In the South; late fifties; before the renaissance of the Black Spirit.

The play takes place in the home of Sue Belle: a two-storied wooden building, aging and rotting from disrepair, dark and somber, a dull green, little space for light, straight, set together in vertical lines, with narrow stairs stuck in to climb from bottom to top, squeezing the space towards the center, seeping upwards to the roof, the rotting tenement buildings surrounding it, shutting out the sun, old men reaching upwards from the grave, mourners all, creating this perpetual night.

SETTING

There are two major playing areas: The upstairs bedroom, upstage and elevated, shared by Sue Belle and Evelina, fronted by a tiny hallway which leads to a doorway U. L. and then offstage to unseen parts of the house, and the downstairs which is a combination living room and kitchen. A simple bannistered stairs connects the two levels.

In the bedroom, there is a wide double bed, a dresser with a mirror, a chest of drawers, a small stool, a small phonograph, a small closet and a night table on which is a lamp of Jesus kneeling in the Garden of Gethsemane. A window and sill holds fifteen dolls of various shapes and sizes. Steps for exit only but not a functional part of the house is U. C. leading from the bedroom offstage; it is only used for the entrance and exit of memory figures and need not be seen by the audience.

In the living room/kitchen, there is a couch, armchair, end table, eating table, a small stove and refrigerator, a large trash can, a door at Left leading outside, and on the wall a picture of "The Last Supper." At the D.L. edge of the stairs is a lunch pail with a doll inside; this remains during the entire play until used by Daddy.

The setting should be stylistic, more impressionistic than expressionistic, projecting a feeling of unreality interjected upon reality, but not to a degree of distortion for with Sue Belle's sickness what is not real is so close to what is real that they cannot be divorced. There will be sound effects which at certain moments in the play will project the same impressionistic effect by being amplified out of proportion to what might be developing on the stage.

My Sister, My Sister

ACT ONE

The play begins. The sound of steady falling rain fills the darkness. There is a voice, a quiet cry from sleep, a gesture, without body.

SUE BELLE. Eddie . . . (*The lights rise slowly, a soft spotlight on* SUE BELLE *as she lifts wearily up in bed. She is only partially dressed in a frayed robe; her hair cut short as if chopped off recently without care, beginning slowly to grow back in an uneven, now uncombed, web about her neck. There is only the sound of rain outside and an occasional car passing. There is little sight, and this pronounces the sounds, intensifying and amplifying them so that they intrude over the glaze of darkness, concrete spectres in themselves.* SUE BELLE *sits up listening, and as she does, there is a crackle of lightning and a rumble of thunder. She speaks to herself, to the emptiness, summoning strength.*) Don't come, Eddie . . . don't come . . . don't come, Eddie . . . Don't . . . Don't let that be his car . . . Rain harder . . . Don't come, Eddie . . . (*A heavy clap of thunder. Searching for some rational base; trying to maintain balance.*) I know I'm makin' yo baby. I can't jus' say stay away . . . What kinda baby that gonna be? All broke out with sores, water-head, people laughin' at him . . . 'Cause a me . . . What kinda Mama am I gonna be? I won't even be able to love ma baby like I need to love him . . . My little dark baby (*Beginning to drift.*) . . . Like Daddy . . . Growin' up into a big dark man like his Daddy . . . I cain't even be sho' no mo' what I'm doin' . . . All these things in ma head

... What kind of mama is ma little black baby gonna have? (*Pause. Offstage,* SPECTRES *hum "Come By Here, Lord."*) Evelina ... Why don't you come home? Mama died with them clappin' and singin', and when they put her in the ground, I wanted to get in too 'cause they jus' won't stop singin' ... Right in the livin' room ... Every night ... And they sing so loud I cain't even think to remember nothin'. I can't figger out nothin'. I can't go to work. I jus' lay up in the bed mos' a the time. Sometime I get the strength to scream out at them but they won't stop comin' inside the house. They know about Eddie, and he's comin' too. I told 'em. They neva lissen to me but they better lissen to Eddie. (SPECTRES' *humming drifts away to nothing.*) Evelina, don't you care what happens to me. ... (*Remembering now; drifting.*) After what you done ... I need to talk to you and now ... now you ain't heah to talk back. ... Eva since I was little, you was like that. ... Eva since. ... But Mama was right about you. ... You neva cared 'bout nobody. You jus' evil.

MAMA. (*Entering from* U. C.—*speaking and moving toward bedroom in darkness.*) Don't you pay no mind to Evelina. The devil done claimed that child. Lord, would you look at you. Yo' hair all fuzzy like a pick-a-patch. Come ova heah, let me comb yo' hair. (*Sits on stool.* SUE BELLE *moves from spotlight into the darkness and while the dialogue continues, the spotlight rises to light the bedroom and* MAMA *and* SUE BELLE [Child]. SUE BELLE [Child] *moves to* MAMA *at stool, sitting at* MAMA'*s feet. Slapping* SUE BELLE *lightly with comb.*) Didn't I tell you not to get all dirty today? We havin' prayer meetin' heah tonight. And 'sides, Miss Beatrice suppose to come ova heah to bring us some things. I don't want you lookin' like no stepchild. (MAMA *begins to brush and comb* SUE BELLE'*s hair, plaiting it in two plaits with two small bows, continuing throughout the following dialogue utnil the action is completed.*)

SUE BELLE (Child). Ow, Mama, dat hurt. Don't do it so hard.

MAMA. Yo' hair too tough . . . I told you to plait it up today. Yo' hair is hard as yo' head.

SUE BELLE (Child). Mama, I didn't do nothin' today.

MAMA. You went to that rock pit today, didn't you?

SUE BELLE (Child). Yes, ma'am.

MAMA. And after I told you not to. People get drownded down there.

SUE BELLE (Child). I didn't mean nothin' bad. Billy and Janie went.

MAMA. Sue Belle, you betta learn to lissen to me. Don't you be so hardheaded like Evelina. Jesus don't like little children who don't lissen to their Mama.

SUE BELLE (Child). Jesus don't mind. Jesus is nice. He ain't gonna drown me in the rock pit.

MAMA. No. He ain't gonna drown you in no rock pit. But if you don't mind, he gonna be mad at you and not love you no mo'.

SUE BELLE (Child). He gonna sic Satan on me?

MAMA. Oh, hush, child!

SUE BELLE (Child). Mama, Jesus ain't like that, is he? He ain't gonna never stop bein' nice to me, is he?

MAMA. (*Hugging her.*) No, Sue Belle, Jesus ain't like that. He jus' like yo' Mama, and He'll always love you 'cause you so sweet. Jus' like a candy apple.

SUE BELLE (Child). Daddy say he gonna take me to the carnibal and buy me a candy apple.

MAMA. He is? . . . Humph! Well . . .

SUE BELLE (Child). (*After a pause.*) I like when you get mad at me, Mama.

MAMA. You like it?

SUE BELLE (Child). It feel real good when you hug me afterwards.

MAMA. Oh hush! (*Swatting her backsides and moves to bed, straightening sheet and dolls at head.*) Now, that's better. You look halfway decent.

SUE BELLE (Child). (*Primping before mirror.*) Long plaits, comb and pick; on my shoulders, lickery sticks!

MAMA. Now don't you get like Evelina and start primpin' in the mirror all the time, thinkin' you're pretty.

SUE BELLE (Child). But I wanta look pretty.

MAMA. You do look pretty. But you ain't supposed to know it . . . Otherwise, that's vanity.

SUE BELLE (Child). What is vanity?

MAMA. Thinkin' 'bout yo' self all the time. (*Moving from bedroom to kitchen/living room.*)

SUE BELLE (Child). (*Following* MAMA.) Well, if I'm by myself all the time, there ain't nobody else to think 'bout. Billy and Janie don't like me 'cause they say I think I'm white like Miss Beatrice. And they don't like to play with me 'cause they say I ain't no fun. (*Sits on daybed.*

MAMA. (*Moving to kitchen table and removing groceries and can goods from paper bag and shelving them.*) That's the devil in Billy and Janie . . .

SUE BELLE (Child). Mama, is the devil colored?

MAMA. Sometimes.

SUE BELLE (Child). Is that why Jesus ain't colored? 'Cause He ain't the devil?

MAMA. Jesus is all colors.

SUE BELLE (Child). Not in my pitcher. Jesus is white jus' like Miss Beatrice.

MAMA. (*Sitting kitchen chair; to* SUE BELLE [Child].) Sue Belle, I'm tryin' to teach you somethin'; so stop askin' so many fool questions. Jesus is all things to everybody but the devil hides himself in black, white, red . . .

SUE BELLE (Child). Blue too, Mama?

MAMA. Well, if there was blue people, he would be but there ain't. So he's all colors that men are. (*Returning to putting up groceries.*) Jus' like a lizard, he changes colors so you can't pick him out from other people. Oh, he's a real slick fella . . . Probably got pressed trousers on, real tight like they wear now, a cap cocked on his head, maybe with sunshades on his eyes, a toothpick in his mouth . . . real sweet words he talks, sweeter than them mangoes Miss Beatrice always brings you . . .

SUE BELLE (Child). Mama, how come the devil don't like nobody?

MAMA. 'Cause he jus' wants us to suffer, that's all.

SUE BELLE (Child). Like when I'm bad and you hit me with the strap?

MAMA. That's chastising.

SUE BELLE (Child). It still hurt.

MAMA. (*Sitting kitchen chair again.*) Child, the devil's hurt is much bigger than that. He makes you hate everybody, thinkin' evil thoughts, not lissenin' to yo' Mama . . . He's slick. He'll make you sick inside till you don't know what you doin' . . . where you at . . . Nothin' . . . And all the time, you think right up till you go screamin' to hell that you got such a fun life.

SUE BELLE (Child). (*Frightened yet fascinated with the horrible images.*) Mama, them fires in hell really burn you? Is that why Evelina burn her hair with that fire-hot comb? Is that Satan that make her face smoke up and her hair sound like chicken fryin' and stinkin' so bad? How come Evelina bring hell in the house? I'm scared of hell.

MAMA. (*Moving to daybed and embracing child.*) Now, honey, you ain't got to be scared a nothin'.

SUE BELLE (Child). But I don't want no devil to burn me . . .

MAMA. Come ovah heah. Sit down wit' yo' Mama.

SUE BELLE (Child). I don't want him to burn Evelina neither. I like Evelina, Mama.

MAMA. Hush up. Hush up now. Now yo' Mama didn't tell you that to scare you. (*A pause as she gathers* SUE BELLE *in.*) When I tell you these things, I jus' want you to know that you should grow up to be good. Come on now . . . hush up now . . . Baby . . .

Baby . . . (*To change the subject.*) Sue Belle, guess what? Guess what I brung for you today?

SUE BELLE (Child). You brung me somethin' today?

MAMA. I sho did. And I want you to guess what it **is**.

SUE BELLE (Child). Guess?

MAMA. That's right.

SUE BELLE (Child). Paper dolls?

MAMA. No.

SUE BELLE (Child). Mangoes?

MAMA. Well, that too. And don't you get them juices all on yo' dress this time.

SUE BELLE (Child). What else?

MAMA. Guess.

SUE BELLE (Child). I done guessed, Mama. Don't tease me.

MAMA. Crayons.

SUE BELLE (Child). Miss Beatrice sent me crayons? Where the bag?

MAMA. Over there on the chair. (SUE BELLE [Child] *runs to the bag on kitchen chair.*)

SUE BELLE (Child). Oooooooo, Mama! They got crazy colors in heah. I didn't know there was so many kinda colors. They got all kinds reds in heah and yellows. What is tookoise? Mama, where the colorin' book you said you was gonna bring me?

MAMA. Wait! You didn't see it all. You so anxious. See. A real big piece of drawin' paper so you kin color big, big pictures.

SUE BELLE (Child). Oh, Mama, Mama, Mama! (*Runs upstairs to bedroom.*)

MAMA. Lord, now I know you ain't gonna leave this room all day . . . (*Laughing pleasantly,* MAMA *leaves kitchen/living room, moves upstairs and walks down the hallway and off Left.* SUE BELLE [Child] *excitedly lays out the large drawing paper on the floor. Then carefully, she lays out the crayons. In the distance, as if separated from this time, there is a sound of a car horn. She sits up listening, confused by the elements which do not fit: The crayons, the rain, her mother. The rain is heard loudly in amplification, followed immediately by repeated honks of a car horn also in amplification.*)

SUE BELLE. Eddddiiieee! (*Another loud blast of a car horn in amplification, and the steady drone of rain.*)

SUE BELLE/EVELINA. Eddie? (*Irritably.*) Eddie!! Goddamnit!!! I wonder why that fool won't come in the house? Eddie, don't be racin' yo' car in the street like you crazy. We got nosey people livin' 'round heah. (*Rising and moving to window.*) Eddie? Eddie? That you ain't it? Look, don't play games wit' me, Nigger! I'm gonna cut you loose, man, if you don't get some sense. You heah me talkin' to you? (*A clap of thunder; She pulls away, terrified with her confusion.*)

SPECTRES. (*Continue into* BILLY's *and* JANIE's *calling.*) Sue Belle . . . Sue Belle . . . Sue Belle . . .

SUE BELLE. Oh, Eddie . . . Eddie . . . Hurry up . . . I need you . . . (*Lifting one of dolls on sill.*) My babies need you . . . I got to figure it out and make it right fo' my babies . . .

MAMA. (*Offstage.*) Sue Belle, it's gettin' dark. You betta get to bed.

BILLY AND JANIE. (*Offstage.*) Sue Belle . . . Hey, Sue Belle . . . You home?

SUE BELLE (Child). Billy? Billy? (*Crosses over to bed and leans out of window.*)

BILLY. (*Offstage.*) Hey, Sue Belle . . .

SUE BELLE (Child). That you, Billy?

BILLY. (*Offstage.*) Who you think it is? Come on down.

SUE BELLE (Child). What for?

BILLY (*Offstage.*) We gonna play some hide-and-go-seek. Janie heah too.

SUE BELLE (Child). I cain't.

JANIE. (*Offstage.*) How come?

SUE BELLE (Child). 'Cause I jus' can't come out.

JANIE. (*Offstage.*) How come? (*Enter* EVELINA

[Adolescent] *from outside door. Throughout the following dialogue, she moves stealthily through the living room, puts books on daybed, goes to icebox and gets glass of milk, then up the stairs and into the bedroom. She is dressed in the teen vogue of the Fifties but with a clumsy attempt at sexuality, perhaps in jeans or tight shorts.*)

SUE BELLE (Child). 'Cause it's gettin' dark.

BILLY. (*Offstage.*) Dark ain't nothin' to be scared of.

SUE BELLE (Child). I jus' cain't come out, Billy.

BILLY. (*Offstage.*) Nobody gonna bother you, girl.

JANIE. (*Offstage.*) Aw, come on, Billy. We kin play by ourselves. How you gonna play hide-and-go-seek with her? You cain't even see her in the dark.

SUE BELLE (Child). I hear you, Janie.

BILLY. (*Offstage.*) Ain't nobody gonna bother you, Sue Belle.

SUE BELLE (Child). You better be careful; all kinda evil come at you in the dark, Billy.

BILLY. (*Offstage.*) Who told you that?

SUE BELLE (Child). My Mama told me that.

BILLY. (*Offstage.*) Yo' Mama ain't told you no such thing.

JANIE. (*Offstage.*) You jus' think you so cute. We don't care if you don't neva come down.

SUE BELLE (Child). How come you say somethin' mean like that, Janie? I wanta come down but my Mama won't let me out at night.

EVELINA (Adolescent). (*In a hushed voice.*) Sue Belle! Sue Belle!

SUE BELLE (Child). Evelina, that you?

BILLY. (*Offstage.*) Hey, Miss Claudine! Kin Sue Belle come out fo' a little while?

EVELINA (Adolescent). 'Course it's me! Don't talk so loud. You wanta git Mama in heah!

SUE BELLE (Child). That's Billy yellin' up eah! (*Puts cigarettes and comic books under mattress.*)

Evelina (Adolescent). Well, git away from that window!

Sue Belle (Child). How come?

Evelina (Adolescent). Don't ask questions, Sue Belle. I don't want Mama in heah preachin'. (*Crosses to phonograph and puts on record: "Blue Moon."*)

Sue Belle (Child). Hey, Billy, I gotta go. (*And to* Evelina [Adolescent].) You jus' gettin' home from school?

Evelina (Adolescent). Yeah.

Sue Belle (Child). How come you jus' gettin' home from school and it's night?

Evelina (Adolescent). (*After glaring at her; a beat.*) Daddy home yet?

Sue Belle (Child). No. He ain't come home yet.

Evelina (Adolescent). Oh, thank God! I don't want Daddy to catch me slippin' in late, thinkin' I'm runnin' 'round with boys.

Sue Belle (Child). Ain't you got a boy friend?

Evelina (Adolescent). Yeah, but I don't want Daddy to know it so don't you go runnin' off at the mouth about it!

Sue Belle (Child). Would Daddy fuss at you?

Evelina (Adolescent). I don' know.

Sue Belle (Child). Well, how come you scared to let him know you got a boy friend?

Evelina (Adolescent). Sue Belle, shit now . . .
(*Simultaneous.*)

Evelina (Adolescent).	Sue Belle (Child).
. . . how come you ask me all these questions all the time?	Oooooooooo! Evelina, you said a bad word!

Evelina (Adolescent). What? What? Shit! I don't know why I had to have a little sister. (Evelina *sits at vanity, opening her books for studying.* Sue Belle [Child] *stands for a bit, and for want of something better to do, she moves to the window sill and sits on bed with her dolls.*)

Sue Belle (Child). Okay, Evelina, I won't bother you. (*To dolls.*) Hey, Tooky, kin you come out to play awhile? . . . No? . . . Where Candy? . . . She went to the sto'? . . . How come we don't all go downstairs and wait for the snowball man to come? (*Giggling.*) Hey, Jacob, what you doin'? (*To* Evelina.) Hey, Evelina, you wanna know what? Jacob sittin' next to Dolly wit' his arms 'round her neck . . . He kissin' her . . .

Evelina (Adolescent). Would you shut up?! I'm studyin'!

Sue Belle (Child). (*A beat pause, recovering from hurt, and then to dolls again.*) When you'll two gonna be married? What you say, Dolly? . . . Well, now, Dolly, you cain't have all the boy friends. You got to leave some for Marsha and Candy and Belinda . . . What you say? (*Giggling.*) You gonna leave her Crazy Ed 'cause he ugly anyway? Dolly, that's not nice. Crazy Ed ain't ugly! He cain't help it 'cause Jesus gave him a hairy face.

Evelina (Adolescent). Sue Belle, please! (*Yelling.*) Mama! Cain't you get me out this room?

Mama. (*Offstage.*) Evelina, you shet up that yellin' in theah!

Evelina (Adolescent). Can't I say nothin' in this house!? (*Rise and cross bedroom door.*)

Mama. (*Offstage.*) Evelina, don't let me come in there at you!

Sue Belle (Child). (*To Dolls.*) You all betta not talk too loud. Evelina got to study. You all go to sleep awhile. (*A long pause as* Sue Belle [Child] *sits quietly watching* Evelina [Adolescent].)

Evelina (Adolescent). Stop starin' at me!

Sue Belle (Child). Don't you like me, Evelina? Don't you like me none at all?

Evelina (Adolescent). Sue Belle . . .

Sue Belle (Child). Ain't you glad to have somebody to talk to? I get lonely all the time if I'm by myself.

EVELINA (Adolescent). (*A long pause as she looks at* SUE BELLE *and then, gently.*) Yeah, I know . . . (*A pause.*) Sue Belle, you jus' got to know that you too little to be keepin' up wit' me . . . I'm fifteen-years-old and you only six.

SUE BELLE (Child). So what?

EVELINA (Adolescent). I'm a soul sister and I got to . . .

SUE BELLE (Child). I want to be yo' soul sister too, Evelina. Kin I? Please!

EVELINA (Adolescent). (*A pause, then sharply.*) You can't!

SUE BELLE (Child). How come?

EVELINA (Adolescent). Because . . . Because . . . You got such a big mouth! Ain't you got enough to talk to with all them things on the windows blockin' out all the fresh air?

SUE BELLE (Child). They ain't things! They my babies!

EVELINA (Adolescent). Yo' what? Yo' babies? No shit! (*Laughing.*) Ain't this a blimp! Girl, where you come from?

SUE BELLE (Child). Stop laughin' at 'em. You hurtin' their feelin's.

EVELINA (Adolescent). Tch! Girl! (*A pause, then quietly.*) How kin I even try to like you? You jus' too stupid. Your babies!

SUE BELLE (Child). I don't have to try to like you. You ma sista.

EVELINA (Adolescent). (*A pause, a long look.*) Shit! Let me go take a bath. (EVELINA *exits from bedroom through hall and offstage Left.* SUE BELLE *sits quietly; presently* JESUS *enters from stage Right, upstairs to bedroom doorway and stands watching her.*)

SUE BELLE (Child). Hey, Jesus. Evelina mad at me again. I don't know why. You wanna see something? (*Moving to crayons and drawing paper.*) See what Miss Beatrice give me. She's really nice. You'd like her.

(*A pause.*) What's the matter? Don't you wanna see these colors? There's a lot of 'em. (*A Pause.*) You still feelin' sad? Ain't you neva gonna be happy? Mama told me how You had two little boys and one 'em killed the other wit' a slingshot. (*A pause.*). How come he done that, Jesus? I mean, You made the sun and everything. Couldn't You make that rock miss? Maybe You got all tired after fixin' the world all up and everything, huh? Don't You neva eat? You awfully skinny. You know what? If the devil wanted to throw me in hell, I don't think You be strong enough to stop him. Yo' arms ain't big like Daddy's. My Daddy'd stop the devil. How come You white people ain't strong? Evelina say that's 'cause you all don't do no work, and colored people like my Daddy got to do all the liftin' and things. (*A pause.*) But You know, Evelina don't like You. She don't like me neither. I don't know why. But I don't think she'd kill me. I mean, you gotta be real bad to do somethin' like that. I don't mean to make You mad by sayin' You little boy is bad . . . but maybe if one of Yo' boys got in trouble, You shoulda whupped him like Mama do me . . . then they woulda minded You and not get killed. (*A pause.*) You know what? I wish You wouldn't be so sad. You make me sad. Hey, I know what? Why don't we play some real good music and You jus' sit and I'll draw Yo' pitcher. (JESUS *crosses to bed and sits.*) That'll make You feel good. I draw real good. My Daddy told me I do. (*Moving to records and phonograph.*) What You wanna hear? Evelina ain't got no church music. (*A pause.*) And what color you want to be? Red or purple? I know. Blue. Blue. Cause Yo' yard in the sky is blue. And Petal got on a blue dress. And the devil is all colors but blue. And Evelina got a real good song called, "Blue . . . Blue . . . Blue Moon." (*Putting on record, "Blue Moon."*) There. (*Returning and settling down to color and draw.*) Now let's see. (*She draws a slow round circle.*) Heah is Yo' face. (*Rising and examining it.*) No. It look kinda lopsided, don't it? You got a real nice face. I'm gonna be careful. (*She retraces it, making the circle rounder.*) There. Now. Eyes. (*Two round circles for eyes.*) Mouth. (*A straight line for mouth.*) No. (*Holding it up in view of audience.*) Now it don't look right, do it? I know why. That's 'cause You still frownin'. Don't You never laugh, Jesus? Ain't You neva gonna be happy? Well, I'm gonna make You happy in ma pitcher. (*Curving up straight line for smile.*) Now. (*Holding it up in view of audience.*) That's real nice. Now I'm gonna put in . . . (*Quick swirly lines.*) Yo' hair on Yo' face. (*Straight line down for body.*) Stomach. (*Upside-down "V" for legs, straight lines for arms and very long, long lines for fingers.*) Fingers. (*A pause.*) I forgot . . . I forgot . . . Mama said You suffered awful on the Cross. I gotta put that in. Right here. (*Huge out of proportion nails, almost as long as the arms, going into the hands with large circles for blood. She rises, pleased with herself, and hangs it on the wall.*) You like it? Huh? Look at it, Jesus. You like it? How come You won't neva smile, Jesus? (*A muffled clap of thunder, a long distance away. The lights begin a slow rise full stage as the* SPECTRES *enter humming "Come By Here, Lord." Simultaneously,* JESUS *rises slowly and exits* U. C. *Unsteadily, lifting a hand to her face and hair.*) How come . . . how come . . . how come God fussin' in the sky? (*The humming of the* SPECTRES *continues.* SUE BELLE *weakens with the flood of images: the crayons,* JESUS, *the rain, and now once again, the haunting chanting of the* SPECTRES. *From both sides of the house, or from the Left and Right wings, the* SPECTRES *begin an entry, a ghost-like processional. One* SPECTRE *holds a tambourine poised in mid-air as if to smash the thunder once again on this frail rotting house. On stage Left, being led on by two* SPECTRES *is also the image of* MAMA, *who is clutching at her breasts, being carried slowly, as if in great distress.* SUE BELLE *is beginning now to once again relive the death and funeral scene of her*

MAMA. *Another* SPECTRE *carries two funeral wreaths which are laid at the* D. R. *edge of daybed.*)

SUE BELLE. (*Struggling for rationality.*) Every time I get things all figgered out, they break apart . . . Ain't nothin' real? Nothin'? But what's in ma head? . . . These things? . . . The rain? . . . All these years . . . In the dark . . . Bunched up . . . Rotten bananas . . . Why did I say that? . . . What about fruit? . . . So strange . . . Meltin' in the sun . . . Breakin' like glass . . . Even when I touch them, they ain't real. And now? What about now? And Daddy? . . . My Daddy . . . Was he ever there? . . . All these little pieces . . . (*The* SPECTRES *move into an uptempo version of "Come by Here," singing the words now, in a frenzied rendition, with hand clapping and dancing. One* SPECTRE *leads* MAMA *to the daybed, and another leans over her fanning her. Another* SPECTRE, *an older male, moves and places his hands in prayer outstretched over* MAMA'S *head. The other* SPECTRES *are clapping and dancing, in their fever and sweat warding off death and Satan.*)

SPECTRES.
> Come by here, Lord!
> Come by here!
> Come by here, Lord!
> Come by here!

SUE BELLE. They here again . . . Please . . . Not tonight . . . Not tonight . . .

SPECTRES.
> Come by here, Lord;
> Come by here!
> Ooooooh, Lord,
> Come by here!

SUE BELLE/EVELINA. (*Sharply, derisively.*) Don't you have nothin' better to do? Who let you in heah? You ain't havin' no wake in heah tonight. Didn't I tell you ma man's comin' ova heah? If you're here when he comes, I'm gonna see wha you' asses are made of, you hear me? You think you can come in heah every night and drive me crazy? Ain't you buried Mama once? Ain't that enough? (*The singing abruptly stops. The* SPECTRES *all turn to stare at her as if they have spoken. A pause as they stare.*) I mean for you to get outta heah! Don't you neva heah nobody? Get out! (*A brief silence. The* SPECTRES *and* MAMA *simultaneously and at their own pace, remove the wreaths and exit from the living room, sinking through the walls into the darkness and offstage.*) Goddamn you, Eddie, keepin' me waitin'. If you're at the Knightbeat gettin' drunk, I'm gonna light yo' ass up like Sterno! And I don't want you tellin' me I got some kind of attitude! Mama and her crazy-ass friends! . . . Ain't nobody in this tomb eva gonna escape . . . Neva . . . (*Moving into the bedroom, she crushes one of the crayons under her foot.*) What is this shit this girl got all ova the flo'? (*A long pause, as she sees the drawing of* JESUS *on the wall.*) Now, we don't need no chaperones tonight, do we, sista? Do we? Ain't gonna be no cryin' outside the do' this time . . . You and me . . . 'Cause yo' mind ain't yo' own . . . Oh, no, 'cause you didn't have to be here when they came . . . Even when I closed the do' you stood listen' . . . You jus' had to know how he breathed and how it sounded . . . how it all was . . . You had to know, so it ain't gonna be no chaperones tonight . . . (*She snatches the drawing from the wall. She puts on a record which is an earthy funky tune, "Honey Love," by the Drifters. She removes the Christ In Prayer Lamp, and then runs downstairs, taking the Praying Hands from end table. She shoves them under the couch and then pauses there looking down at it.*) Ma night, Mama . . . Ma night . . . Let's get some fresh air in this place . . . (*She moves to front door; opens it.*) Hhmmm! That's so good . . . So good . . . I hope you're all out there, you heah me? I hope you propped up with yo' spy glasses. You betta dig this drive-in movie. You ain't got to pay fo' my kinda action. It's in color on a wide-ass screen. Look what you get for nothin' . . . This is ma night tonight . . . (*Laughing now.*) "Ain't gonna be no problem." (*Moving back into room, memories and voices attack.*)

EVELINA (Adult Taped Voice). What time is Mama comin' home?

SUE BELLE (Adolescent Taped Voice). Mama is in Jacksonville.

SUE BELLE. (*Coming apart, quietly, summoning strength.*) No problem, Mama . . .

EVELINA (Adult Taped Voice). Did she take her robe?

SUE BELLE (Adolescent Taped Voice). She ironed it befo' she left and put it in a shopping bag . . .

SUE BELLE. My night, Mama . . . The blackest man I could find . . . You couldn't know how black . . . sof' like satin . . . He holds me and his mouth don't let me scream . . . His arms 'round me, his movin' me, singin' out ma name, sayin' good things with his Sue Belle . . . I don't move . . . He don't let me . . . 'Cause ain't nothin' real . . . Ain't nothin' right but Eddie . . . It's ma night, Mama . . . I'm gonna have it . . . (*She climbs stairs quickly and moves into bedroom.*) Evelina, where did I put comb and hot plate . . . I'm gonna look nice fer you, Eddie . . . (*She fumbles at vanity, finds hot plate, comb, curling iron, pressing grease. She sits down and sets it up.*) Things gonna change . . . Not no mo' . . . In and outa this house like this was a whore house . . . All them men . . . So many I forget, Evelina . . . But them last ones . . . How many? . . . Three or four? . . . And that last one, Evelina . . . That last one . . . Jesus . . . When you ran out bleeding from Mama's strap, how come you didn't take all this stuff with you . . . I can't do it like you . . .

EVELINA (Adult). (*In darkness.*) I'm sorry you always here, sister . . . (*Lights slowly begin to rise, revealing* EVELINA [Adult]. *She is dressed in black half slip and black strapless bra. Entering from* U. S. *door. Her hair has been straightened and curled; this should be a wig.*) You can't live in this house. (*Sits on bed.*) It's like a old old man always watchin', mournin' . . . Jealous'a whoever comes in . . . Pass me that hot comb, Sue Belle . . . Sometimes at night, I hear these walls talkin' to me . . . They always talk about dyin' . . . Sue Belle, did you heah me . . . Would you stop moppin' and give me the comb . . . (*Taking comb from her.*) You'd be late for your own funeral . . . (*Touching up curls with hot curlers and comb.*) Girl, you better get some life in you . . . You a big girl now, you know that . . . And Goddamnit, girl, tell Mama not to be plaitin' up yo' hair. (*Rising and moving to* SUE BELLE *at vanity; she removes bows from* SUE BELLE's *hair.*) You twelve years old. You ain't gonna neva get no man lookin' like Topsy . . .

SUE BELLE (Adolescent). I don't want no man. (SUE BELLE (Adolescent) *rises and sits on bed, while* EVELINA [Adult] *sits at vanity.*)

EVELINA (Adult). Humph! You sho' awfully curious all the time . . . And I know you, you don't want to end up no used-up whore like me . . .

SUE BELLE (Adolescent). Why you talk 'bout yo'self like that?

EVELINA (Adult). The truth is the light, baby. What you think Mama call me? Snow White? Cinderella? Shit! I'm known to have me several little dwarfs in the closet. (*Knocking on closet wall laughing.*)

SUE BELLE (Adolescent). Oh, shut up!

EVELINA (Adult). Oh, don't bullshit me, girl. This is Evelina, remember? I know you! Every time I have a little company I see how you look at me.

SUE BELLE (Adolescent). Well, you don't have to bring 'em heah.

EVELINA (Adult). But I do, don't I? . . . And every time, you watchin' and takin' names. You look jus' like Mama. You even sound jus' like Mama. Sometimes I think if you would jus' close yo' eyes . . . Jus' once . . . I might be able to fool myself 'bout what I really am . . . But jus' like I can't get outa this house, I can't get outa yo' eyes . . . Even when I'm long gone, I think I'll still be heah . . . Those last two times . . . I don't even know why I did it . . . Them white men, I can't stand 'em . . . But I do it, and sometimes I'm sorry afterwards but I do it . . .

SUE BELLE (Adolescent). You don't have to . . . You don't love them . . .

EVELINA (Adult). Love! I don't know what all that means. That love shit, you gotta get that to give it . . . or even to know what it is . . . No, sista, you gotta lay that love shit aside. It'll get yo' mind all messed up. You jus' get the right color dress and a sof', sof' material too so a man can feel you through it, then when he's begun to touch more of you, that love shit will take care of itself . . . (*Moving to closet.*) The right color . . . Like this one . . . And that one . . . This red one. You want him to taste you, cherry sweet, soft, brown, sugar cinnamon cake, chocolate icing, strawberry mouth . . . But wit' his eyes first . . . 'Cause if a man fills up wit' you too fast, he goes to sleep and there ain't nothin' satisfyin' in that. Dreams are cold. But if you do what I tell you now, things gonna be fine. Ain't nothin' gonna satisfy his sweet tooth like you . . . He'll be yo' man anytime you want him and you won't neva need . . . anytime it's rainin', or when you want to tell Mama to go to hell 'cause you're sick of bein' crazy and by yo'self, or when you go to bed and you need his arms to crawl into, he'll be there. That's what you dress for . . . that's why you make that sof' red dress cling tight to yo' tits, shape yo' ass. That's why you wear orange and chartreuse and pink and red, but not no white . . . To hell with Miss Beatrice and her cold, clammy, tight-assed skin . . . You're alive and you need colors to strut yo' stuff . . . Brown Spanish lime, pop with the skin, juices, sweet juices; he's squeezin' you all ova . . . . Strut yo' stuff! Make yo' hips turn, twist . . . Strut it . . . Legs dancing, criss-crossing, tits shinin' high, light yo' way! Say, "Heah, I come baby!" Sway yo' shoulders . . . Fine to death! Be fine! You know he ain't goin' no where! Orange lipstick! Draw in yo' eyes so they're a cat watchin' him from the inside; he can't stand that kind of voodoo . . . Tellin' him what to do to you . . . Tellin' him, "Can't I mess wit' yo' mind, baby, if I want to . . . Can't I make yo' do ma thing when I'm ready . . . Anytime I feel like it . . . On my time . . . If I feel like it . . . Gonna give it to you" . . . Say, "Come on, Daddy, make me feel good . . . My time . . . It's ma time now . . . Oh shit! Jus' don't stop, Daddy! Oh, Daddy! Shit now! Do it to me!" (EVELINA [Adult], *continues her moaning, her hips and thighs swaying. Atop her sounds, taped voices speak out in amplification.*)

EVELINA (Adult). (*Amplified.*) What time is Mama comin' home?

SUE BELLE (Adolescent). (*Amplified.*) Mama is in Jacksonville.

EVELINA (Adult). (*Amplified.*) Did she take her robe?

SUE BELLE (Adolescent). (*Amplified.*) She ironed it befo' she left and put it in a shopping bag.

SUE BELLE (Adolescent). Evelina, why you lie to me? (*A beat pause; cut tapes.*)

EVELINA (Adult). Ain't nothin' a lie, Sister Virgin. This shit is real.

SUE BELLE (Adolescent). You said you were sorry, but you ain't. You ain't sorry about nothin' . . . You ain't neva sorry . . . You got to feel for somebody to be sorry. You neva cared nothin' 'bout me . . . 'bout Mama . . . 'bout . . .

EVELINA (Adult). Well? Go on and say it! You Argo-starched bitch, say it!

SUE BELLE (Adolescent). (*Fighting back.*) I ain't gonna say nothin'!

EVELINA (Adult). 'Cause you can't even think that lie! You know I loved Daddy. He was the first fuckin' man I ever loved.

SUE BELLE (Adolescent). Evelina, what you sayin'?!

EVELINA (Adult). Oh, shut up! Shut up! And stop starin' at me! You ain't no better! Always crawlin' up into his arms and huggin' him and kissin' him and pettin' him! You little bitch, you was a whore befo' I even knew the word. Now suffer with that!

SUE BELLE (Adolescent). You make everybody suffer, Evelina, when it ain't their fault.

EVELINA (Adult). No shit! Now, ain't this a bitch! You don't know what sufferin' is.

SUE BELLE (Adolescent). With all the stuff you been tellin' me? All the things you been doing! Bring them white men up heah! You make me sick!

EVELINA (Adult). You ain't sick yet!

SUE BELLE (Adolescent). (*Fighting back.*) Turn me loose, Evelina.

EVELINA (Adult). Not yet you ain't! You ain't suffered yet! You ain't cried yet! You ain't been drunk yet! You ain't even been fucked yet. Oh, no, Sue Belle, I hate yo' ass too much for jus' a few tears to turn me off. Jus' one mo' time! . . . One mo' night! . . . Now tell me . . . (*Loudly.*) What time is Mama comin' home?

SUE BELLE (Adolescent) Oh, Jesus, no! Turn me loose.

EVELINA (Adult). You heah me talkin' to you, Sista Virgin?

SUE BELLE (Adolescent). Evelina, I can't make up fer Daddy. I'm sorry 'bout yo' babies . . . I'm sorry you drowned 'em . . . I'm sorry Mama whipped you . . .

EVELINA (Adult). I asked you a question, Sista Virgin!!!!

Sue Belle (Adolescent). (*Quietly monotone.*) What . . . What . . . What did you ask me?

Evelina (Adult). What time is Mama comin' home?

Sue Belle (Adolescent). Mama is in Jacksonville, Evelina.

Mama. (*Entering from* u. c. *across landing, downstairs and into living room. She carries a robe, shopping bag and suitcase.*) Sue Belle, I'm goin' now. (*A pause.* Sue Belle *is slipping, becoming more and more unsteady.*)

Sue Belle. But . . . But Mama ain't supposed to be heah . . .

Evelina (Adult). Well, look at me . . . Ain't I heah, sista?

Sue Belle. I don't know . . . I don't know . . .

Evelina (Adult). Did she take her robe?

Sue Belle. What?

Evelina (Adult). Did she take her robe? (*A long pause.*)

Sue Belle (Adolescent). She ironed it befo' she left and put it in a shopping bag.

Mama. (*Folding robe and slipping it in the shopping bag.*) Sue Belle, you upstairs?

Evelina (Adult). Jus' remember what I tol' you, sister Sue Belle. You strut yo' stuff tonight. Shake yo' money maker. (*She exits upstage door.*)

Mama. Sue Belle!

Sue Belle (Adolescent). I'm comin', Mama. (Sue Belle [Adolescent] *crosses out of bedroom to stair landing.* Mama *is waiting in kitchen holding a small cardboard suitcase and a shopping bag. She is dressed in a faded outdated dress in a glaringly tasteless print.*) Heah I am, Mama.

Mama. What took you so long? I been callin' you seems like an hour now. Why you tremblin' so?

Sue Belle (Adolescent). (*Struggling to hold back tears; refusing to cry.*) Nothin'.

Mama. Don't lie to me, Sue Belle.

SUE BELLE (Adolescent). Oh, Mama, I wouldn't!
MAMA. Well, what's ailin' you?
SUE BELLE (Adolescent). Huh?
MAMA. Sue Belle!
SUE BELLE (Adolescent). Mama, ain't nothin' wrong with me.
MAMA. You and Evelina been fightin' again?
SUE BELLE (Adolescent). Ma'am?
MAMA. Sue Belle, I don't feel like standin' up heah talkin' like no echo.
SUE BELLE (Adolescent). It was my fault, Mama. I jus' . . . I jus' broke one of her records.
MAMA. Well, why did you do that?
SUE BELLE (Adolescent). I jus' dropped it.
MAMA. You tell her it was a accident.
SUE BELLE (Adolescent). Ma'am?
MAMA. Did you tell her it was a accident, Sue Belle?
SUE BELLE (Adolescent). Mama, don't look at me so hard.
MAMA. Well, you ain't tellin' me the truth? I told you and told you 'bout lyin'.
SUE BELLE (Adolescent). Mama, you frighten me when you look at me like that.
MAMA. Now, lissen, Sue Belle, I'm gonna ask you for the last time and if you want me to get that strap out that closet, I sho' will. I don't mean for you to get in the habit of lyin' 'round this house. Hol' yo' head up! You heah me talkin' to you?
SUE BELLE (Adolescent). (*Breaking into tears.*) Yes, ma'am, I don't mean to lie.
MAMA. You go up and tell Evelina to bring herself down heah right this minute.
SUE BELLE (Adolescent). (*Runs downstairs into living room.*) No, Mama . . . No . . . Please . . . It was ma fault, Mama! You know when I'm dreamin' I neva thinka nothin'! And Evelina was right. She spent eighty cents for that record. Please don't fuss at Evelina 'cause a me.

MAMA. Tch! Child! (*She pulls* SUE BELLE [Adolescent] *into her arms.*) If that's all it was, that ain't no reason to be cryin'. (*A long pause as* SUE BELLE *hugs* MAMA *tightly.*)

SUE BELLE (Adolescent). Oh, Mama . . . (*A long pause as rocking and hugging subsides.*)

MAMA. Next time don't be beatin' 'round the bush. You come right out and tell me the truth straight out. (MAMA *lifts bag and suitcase and begins to walk out.* SUE BELLE *stands apart now, as if having been released too soon, unprepared, cold, wanting more.*)

SUE BELLE (Adolescent). You ought to whip me good for bein' so careless.

MAMA. Do what? Whip you? For breakin' a record? One of them dirty songs that I keep tellin' her not to play in the house anyway? The things you talk! Now come on, give me a kiss. I gotta go.

SUE BELLE (Adolescent). Evelina, Mama goin'. Better come downstairs! Evelina, hurry up!

MAMA. You worry 'bout Evelina more'n Evelina worries about herself. That's a waste of time. You kin preach and preach all you want to that hardheaded girl. She twenty-one years old now and too much of a woman. Her and her Knightbeat! Both of 'em gonna go straight to hell.

SUE BELLE (Adolescent). Give me another hug, Mama.

MAMA. Sue Belle, I gotta run . . . I'm gonna be late.

SUE BELLE (Adolescent). You neva hug me 'less you mad at me.

MAMA. (*Jokingly, teasing in a kind of pouting tone.*) Well, what you wanna do to make me mad at you?

SUE BELLE (Adolescent). Mama, you makin' jokes.

MAMA. Sue Belle, what's ailin' you tonight?

SUE BELLE (Adolescent). I don't know, Mama. I jus' feel strange about tonight. I don't know why. I jus' don't want you goin' to Jacksonville. Me and Evelina gonna be home by ourselves. And . . . I don't know. I jus' got these feelin's.

MAMA. You stop that poutin'. You twelve years old now. You ain't no baby. You know why I gotta go to Jacksonville.

SUE BELLE (Adolescent). (*Crosses. Sits at kitchen table.*) Yeah, Mama . . . I know . . . I jus' . . . Well, okay . . . Don't pay no mind to me. I guess I jus' don't feel good, that's all. You have a good time. You eat yo' dinner?

MAMA. I ain't been hungry.

SUE BELLE (Adolescent). You been workin' all day. Ain't you gonna be weak if you don't eat? You been sick, Mama, and the doctor already tol' you you got to get some rest wit' them pains in yo' chest.

MAMA. Doctor! Doctor! Don't tell me nothin' 'bout no doctor!

SUE BELLE (Adolescent). But, Mama, you can't even sleep in Reverend Johnson's beat-up car bouncing you all around.

MAMA. Lord, it do that alright! When I get out that car, I feel shook up like a cornbread batter. But what can I do? That's all we got to move in, and if in doin' God's work, I had to ride a mule, I'd ride him. I ain't better'n . . . Jesus.

SUE BELLE (Adolescent). (*Still concerned.*) Mama . . .

MAMA. Oh, stop worryin', child. (*A brief pause.*) Sue Belle? Sue Belle, how come you shakin' like that? What is wrong with you? You gettin' sick? What happened up there? (*Calling.*) Evelina, you bring yo'self right down here . . . this minute! What you done to this child? Come down heah! (*Pacing; a pause.*) Maybe I ought not to go to Jacksonville. You really don't look good. Come on, and lay yo'self down on this couch. (*Steering* SUE BELLE *to couch.*) I'm gonna make you some hot tea befo' I go. And when I come back, I'm gonna boil you up some serasee.

SUE BELLE (Adolescent). Aaaaaagh! That stuff taste awful.

MAMA. Well, you gonna take some. Clean yo' system out. Come on, lay down.

SUE BELLE (Adolescent). No, Mama, you go on. I'm alright.

MAMA. (*Lightly.*) Well, I'm sho' Reverend Johnson probably ain't even come yet.

SUE BELLE (Adolescent). I already put some water on to boil.

MAMA. What for? You boilin' water for a bath? The water heater gone out again?

SUE BELLE (Adolescent). I jus' thought you might want some coffee or somethin' befo' you go.

MAMA. Well, I like that. Don't you neva get tired a workin'? Besides, don't be givin' me orders. You may hold this family together but you ain't the boss.

SUE BELLE (Adolescent). I cook the dinner every night.

MAMA. (*Lightly.*) Yeah, I know how you cook yo' pigeon peas and rice chews like oatmeal.

SUE BELLE (Adolescent). Mama, tell me 'bout Jacksonville. Tell me what you do up there.

MAMA. Jacksonville?

SUE BELLE (Adolescent). That's so far to go off preachin'.

MAMA. Sue Belle, I don't have time now.

SUE BELLE (Adolescent). Tell me, Mama, I want to know.

MAMA. Sue Belle . . .

SUE BELLE (Adolescent). Please, Mama!

MAMA. Well, child, it's been more than jus' Jacksonville. We been all up and down this state. Into Georgia, too. There's a whole lotta people need savin' in this world. A whole lot! At night, we have prayer meetin' with preachin' and singin' and testifyin', and then comes mornin', we're up at six and out on the street, talkin' to people as they go to work, to anybody that'd listen. We preach and pray for them. If they're in a hurry, we jus' give them prayers for the day. Some of those mornings, it's so beautiful . . . the air so fresh . . . the people, although they been sufferin', they still be tryin' to make it through another day . . . hopin' like colored people got to hope that this day, it's gonna be better . . . I do love to reach out to them, to do my small part in helpin' them meet my sweet saviour Jesus.

SUE BELLE (Adolescent). Oh, Mama, that's so beautiful. How you feel about Jesus is so beautiful.

MAMA. At night at Prayer Meetin', I can't believe sometimes the love that takes ahold of us. People shoutin' and testifyin' . . . Oh, we ain't got no fancy tents or big churches with them curly roofs and gold and high towers. Jus' somebody's grocery sto' or maybe somebody's house. But, Sue Belle, when Jesus comes into that room . . . My Lord! . . . "In my Father's House there are many mansions," He said. And you can feel it! The richness of His love! You look over at yo' neighbor and it's like you kin just reach over and touch his heart. You kin feel his sufferin' and you know that he's bleedin' 'cause he's jus' like you, and his blood is yo' blood 'cause you are both floatin' in the blood of Jesus.

SUE BELLE (Adolescent). Oh, yes, Mama!

MAMA. You know He's there!

SUE BELLE (Adolescent). Oh, yes, Mama, I know He's there!

MAMA. (*Rises to center stage.*) It makes you wanna shout, clap yo' hands . . . Sometimes I feel like I'm floatin' up there, far above myself with Jesus. My feet don't wanna touch the ground. I seen a blind man get his sight back, a woman who ain't been able to talk in ten years suddenly shout out, "Help me, Jesus. You know You are my Shepherd; I shall not want!" . . . Young and old . . . Even white folks come . . . Reverend Johnson places his hands on them . . . and then, black on white, you know Jesus is the spirit of love.

Sue Belle (Adolescent). Did that really happen, Mama? Oh, I wish I could go jus' once to see it. I know Him, Mama! I know Him! I see Him all the time! He comes and sits with me all the time. Sometimes I want to hold Him so tight I don't want to never turn Him loose. I want to be like you and go preachin' and testifyin'.

Mama. Don't you know I know the feelin' . . . Don't you know it, Sue Belle. Sometimes I think how I could've jus' withered away when your Daddy left. Remember, I couldn't sleep . . . Runnin' fevers all the time . . . Pains in ma chest . . . No reason for livin' . . . That Satan, he had his claws in ma heart . . . Lord, he did! Couldn't see nothin' but myself. Selfishness . . . That's the worst sin . . . But you see, even when I was a child, much younger than you are now, it broke my heart when someone I loved walked out without a word . . . even when they turned out to be different than what I thought . . . Sometimes, I would crawl in a closet and sit there on a heap of dirty clothes, cryin' in the darkness. Couldn't catch ma breath sometimes in the stale air . . . but day would change to night befo' I stopped and come out . . . And I was weak for days after . . . (*A Pause.*) Lord, I love too hard! And that's a sin too, I guess. 'Cause Satan waited there . . . He plotted and waited and waited and waited there . . . that evil snake crawled up from his black pit . . . Lucifer from his hell . . . Crawlin' from his black pit of despair . . . Reachin' out, grabbin' me, turnin' me around and around, every way but loose!

Sue Belle (Adolescent). Preach it, Mama!

Mama. Satan made me cry out, "Who gonna love me now? Who gonna take care of me now?" . . . Had no thoughts of Jesus! Had turned ma back on Jesus! I shoulda climbed down on my knees and screamed out through ma blind black darkness and despair . . . Shoulda screamed out, "Jesus, show me the light! Fire up ma heart so that I can love again!" But no, that

Satan stood too near. I had opened the door of ma heart and there Satan stood blockin' the path of ma saviour Jesus. Satan said, "Womaaaaaaaaaan! Woman! What has Jesus done for you today?" I'm talkin' to you now! He said, "How loooooooong you gonna suffer for that unfeelin' Jesus? How looooooooong you gonnnna tote His heavy cross? Don't you get tired sometime, woman? How long?"

SUE BELLE (Adolescent). How long, Mama? How long?

MAMA. I said, "As loooooooooong, Satan, as Jesus gives me air to breathe, I'm gonna serve Him!" I said, "As loooooooooooong as Jesus gives me tears I'm gonna cry for Jesus and cry and cry and shed His blood. 'Cause sufferin' for Jesus is a lovin' thing.

SUE BELLE (Adolescent). Suffer for Jesus, Mama!

MAMA. One night it was . . . Night as black as sin . . . I saw the light of Jesus walkin' 'cross this room . . . He stood befo' me . . . a fire where there was no light . . . Holdin' out His hands to me . . . His voice like soft cool hands across my face . . . washin' my sins away . . . My Lord, He stepped ova . . . And my Saviour, my Rock, my Strength shouted out, "Get back, Satan! This woman has suffered enough!" He said, "Step baaaaaaack, Satan! This good woman belongs to My Father."

SUE BELLE (Adolescent). Preach it, Mama!

MAMA. How I cried! Yes I did! I cried, "Jesuuuuuuus, show me the way! Tell me what You want me to do. If You want me to die, take ma hand. If You want me to suffer . . .

SUE BELLE (Adolescent). Suffer for Jesus, Mama!

MAMA. . . . take ma hand! If You want me to be blind, crippled, filled with sores from ma head to ma feet, take ma hand. I'll crawl with You, Jesus! Jus' show me what You want me to do!

SUE BELLE (Adolescent). Preach! Preach! Oh ma Lord, preach!

MAMA. Lord, I was tremblin' so . . . a pain cuttin' ma breath as sharp as death . . . Tears runnin' down my cheeks . . . Couldn't breathe . . . Fillin' ma head with light, a brightness forever shinin', more lasting than death . . . Couldn't breathe . . . Choked with sin . . . Throwin' up Satan's dry cold bones of sin and death . . Throwin' it up, Jesus . . . Take me, Lord, take me! . . . Like a cool rain on a day scorched from the flames of hell, Jesus said, "Fear not, woman, I am with you eveeeeeeeeeeeen till the ends of the earth."

SUE BELLE (Adolescent). Oh Lord, Mama. Take me with You, Lord. Take me with You!

MAMA. No mo' pain!

SUE BELLE (Adolescent) AND SPECTRES. Take me with You!

MAMA. No mo' sufferin'!

SUE BELLE (Adolescent) AND SPECTRES. Take me with You!

MAMA. Didn't feel no hunger!

SUE BELLE (Adolescent) AND SPECTRES. Take me with You!

MAMA. No mo' thinkin' 'bout myself, 'bout my troubles, 'bout this, 'bout that . . . Didn't feel Satan's hands, black as death, curled around my heart . . . Jesus stepped in! Yes, He did!

SUE BELLE (Adolescent) AND SPECTRES. Yes, He did!

MAMA. Led me down the paths of righteousness for His name's sake!

SUE BELLE (Adolescent) AND SPECTRES. Yes.

MAMA. He was ma rock . . . my solid ground . . . Turned me around . . . You know You did, Jesus!

SUE BELLE (Adolescent). Save me! Save me, Mama! Save me from the cross!

MAMA. I said, "Jesuuuuuuuuuuuus, You are my . . .

SPECTRES. Yes!

MAMA. I said, "Jesuuuuuuuuuuuus, You are my . . .

SPECTRES. Yes!

MAMA. I said, "Jesuuuuuuuuuuus, You are my rock, my solid rock, I'm callin', Jesus . . .

SPECTRES. My rock!

MAMA. Callin', Jesus!

SPECTRES. My Rock!

MAMA. Callin' Jesus!

SPECTRES. My Rock! (SPECTRES *enter singing "Come By Here." Up tempo. One* SPECTRE *leads* MAMA *to daybed, in a flash of the scene from* SUE BELLE'S *past when* MAMA *sat dying from heart attack. This scene in tempo, movement and picturization is identical to the one which occurred earlier in the act. One* SPECTRE *fans* MAMA; *another* SPECTRE, *an older male, moves to pray over the suffering* MAMA. *The others clap and dance as they ward off death and Satan. A heavy clap of thunder.*)

SUE BELLE. (*After a pause. Moves quickly off day bed to steps.*) No, Mama! (SPECTRES *bring in two small funeral wreaths which are placed* D. R. *of daybed.*)

EDDIE. (*Offstage.*) Hey, baby, it's me! (*There is a sharp knock on the door. The* SPECTRES *all turn to* MAMA, *who sits quite still, staring outwards.*)

SUE BELLE. (*To* SPECTRES.) I tol' you he was comin'. I tol' you. (SUE BELLE *moves over on stairs.*) Eddie! Eddie! Wait a minute! Mama, please this once, let it be different. (*A pause.*)

EDDIE. (*Offstage.*) Hey, baby! You pissed off, huh? They all flooded out on 14th Street. Got tied up in that traffic and I couldn' get out. I got stalled . . . Hey, baby!

SUE BELLE. Oh, Jesus, no!

EDDIE. (*Offstage.*) You want me to break this do' down? I'm gettin' all wet out heah! Woman, open this do'! You hear me? Open this God-damned do'! (*A beat pause, and* JESUS *exits.*)

SUE BELLE. Mama . . . I ain't gonna watch it no

more. You hear me? I ain't! (*The* Spectres *remove the funeral wreaths, separate, and exit through walls. A beat pause;* Mama *looks at her, stands and then exits Right.*) I'm comin', Eddie . . . (*She opens door.*) Eddie . . .

Eddie. (*As he enters.*) Look at this shit, willya? Man, I feel . . . Well, ain't you gonna get me a towel or somethin'? . . . Damn! (*A pause; watching her.*) What is it, baby?

Sue Belle. Hold me, Eddie . . . Hold me . . .

Eddie. (*Pulling her into his arms.*) You gonna let a little thunder worry you, baby?

Sue Belle. I can't help it. It's too much like that clappin' and singin'.

Eddie. Yeah, I dig where you comin' from, baby. My man upstairs is havin' hisself one boss set.

Sue Belle. Don't say that. You scare me to death when you talk like that. (*Crosses and sits on daybed.*)

Eddie. (*Laughing..*) Alright, baby! (*Taking off his coat and cap; circling the living room.*) So this is yo' pad. You know, you told me so much about it I can jus' see yo' Mama standing there with her scissors.

Sue Belle. Eddie, hold me.

Eddie. Don't worry, baby. I'm takin' care of you. Ma pad might be small but it's ready. We gonna have ten little picky heads running 'round cryin' for their mama.

Sue Belle. I know . . . I know, Eddie . . . That's what scares me . . . They were pushed out the window, all fifteen . . . They drowned in all that rain.

Eddie. Come here, baby. (*She crosses to him and he kisses her.*)

Sue Belle. (*She freezes.*) Oh, Eddie . . .

Eddie. Hey, hey, what is this? Is this the same fiery bitch I been screwin' for two years? (*He kisses her again.*) What you tryin' to do, baby? You learnin' all ova again about kissin'? Or you savin' yo' tongue for talkin'? (*A pause.* Sue Belle *looks up at him, leans into him, pressing gently. Slowly* SUE BELLE/EVELINA *lifts up to his lips.*)

SUE BELLE/EVELINA. And what you savin', Eddie, Eddie, Boss Black and Ready!

EDDIE. I ain't no bank, baby.

SUE BELLE/EVELINA. You my bank! So jus' save it!

EDDIE. Till when, Mama?

SUE BELLE/EVELINA. Till I call for it! Don't I always? (*She turns sharply and moves toward steps. She stops momentarily staring up at bedroom.*)

EDDIE. Hey, Mama, you don't give me no chance for my comeback! Hey! (SUE BELLE/EVELINA *moves quickly up the stairs.*) What's the matter with you? Where you goin'?

SUE BELLE/EVELINA. (*Takes off robe, throws it on the floor.*) On ma time, Daddy . . . When I'm ready . . . (*Moves into bedroom. Intense.*) This is my night, Mama, this is my night!

BLACKOUT

ACT TWO

At the opening of the act, Eddie is seated on the chair stuffing a sandwich into his mouth. Sue Belle/ Evelina enters from upstairs bedroom. Sue Belle/Evelina moves down the stairs into the living room. She wears that red dress now, a carbon of Evelina's. Her hair has been combed, and brushed and greased and straightened to a sheen. Her face is heavily made-up. She stands momentarily at top of stair landing waiting for Eddie to see her and admire her.

Eddie. Hey, Sue Belle! Damn, baby! What took you so long?

Sue Belle/Evelina. I see you been makin' good use of yo' time.

Eddie. Yeah, baby. I can put away some food.

Sue Belle/Evelina. (*Moves downstairs to clear food from table.*) You eat like a hog. Don't know what I see in you.

Eddie. (*Crosses to her.*) My smoke sausage!

Sue Belle/Evelina. Go smoke yo' ass. And get outa my way. (*Beat pause.*) And stop stuffin yo' face; I don't work to feed you. (*A long pause.*)

Eddie. You go upstairs, stay a whole hour, what you expect me to do? (*Moving to table.*) Keep yo' damn food!

Sue Belle/Evelina. Hey, man!

Eddie. (*Crosses back to chair stage Left.*) What the hell you want?

Sue Belle/Evelina. Where you think you goin'?

Eddie. From this wall to this wall! Stupid ass ques-

39

tion! Where the hell do you think I'm goin' in all this rain?

SUE BELLE/EVELINA. I ain't thinkin', baby. Not now. (*A pause.*) Look at me, Eddie. Turn around. (*A pause.*) Now . . . Am I fine? Hhhhmmm? Do I turn you on? (EDDIE *lights a cigarette.*)

SUE BELLE/EVELINA. Do you want me now, baby? Hhhmmm?

EDDIE. Look, Sue Belle! Don't play with me.

SUE BELLE/EVELINA. I ain't playin' witchu. You aint no doll. You ma man, aint you?

EDDIE. I don't know what I am to you. I nearly drown to get ova heah to you and then what? You disappear upstairs for ova an hour. And then you wont even let me upstairs when I ask you. "Just stay downstairs, Eddie, just stay downstairs!" Shit! You think I wanna hang around this place all night? I don't want your Mama comin' down here at me wit' no scissors.

SUE BELLE/EVELINA. (*Laughing.*) Why should she do that? You aint no girl.

EDDIE. What does that have to do with it? I can bleed.

SUE BELLE/EVELINA. So can I! (*A pause.*)

EDDIE. I need a drink. What you got to drink? (*He sits in chair Stage Left.*)

SUE BELLE/EVELINA. (*Laughing.*) You mean you aint even bought a bottle, cheap ass nigger? (*She sits in kitchen chair stage Right.*)

EDDIE. Damn! Why you wanta keep comin' down on me like that?

SUE BELLE/EVELINA. 'Cause you aint shit! You greedy! You lazy! And besides you don't know nothin' 'bout love and about how to treat a woman. Nothin'!

EDDIE. Shit, I know a lotta women be ready to jump for Eddie!

SUE BELLE/EVELINA. I jus' bet you do!

EDDIE. Oh, to hell with you! I'm goin' home. (*Rises to leave.*)

SUE BELLE/EVELINA. Guess you goin' to go to one of yo' other women, huh?
EDDIE. You damn right I'm goin'. You watch me.
SUE BELLE/EVELINA. Well, fine. Go to yo' other woman.
EDDIE. I will! That aint no big thing!
SUE BELLE/EVELINA. (*Crosses to him stage Left then sits on daybed.*) I hope that she buys a new dress to look special for you. And I hope she sits in front of a goddamned mirror cookin' her hair and paintin' her face over and over so she can impress you. And I hope you can at least tell her that she looks half-way good to you. Not all the way, you cold son-of-a-bitch! Jus' half-way! I hope so!
EDDIE. Oh, goddamnit! Shit!
SUE BELLE/EVELINA. Good night, Eddie.
EDDIE. Look, I . . . Baby . . . I'm sorry. Sue Belle, wait a minute. Come on now, honey. You look boss. You know you always look boss to me.
SUE BELLE/EVELINA. Don't touch me. I mean it, Eddie. Son of a bitch! Get all you can from yo' other woman, you hear! You don't touch me no mo', Eddie.
EDDIE. Sue Belle, you know I don't have no other woman.
SUE BELLE/EVELINA. I don't know nothin'.
EDDIE. Baby, I eat, sleep and drink thinking of you. You don't leave no space in ma brains fer nobody else.
SUE BELLE/EVELINA. I been wonderin' how to get rid of you anyway.
EDDIE. You don't mean that.
SUE BELLE/EVELINA. I do too mean it. I can't stand the sight of you. You make me sick. (*A long pause.*)
EDDIE. Yeah, I bet I do. (*He moves to her and kisses her.*) Does that change yo' mind?
SUE BELLE/EVELINA. Don't play wit' me! If you gonna kiss me, kiss me. Don't be playin' no damned 20 questions wit' me.
EDDIE. Give a break, baby. I was jus' sellin' wolf

tickets. You know how I talk. (*A pause.*) Baby, I been workin' all day in that hot-ass laundry room . . .

Sue Belle/Evelina. So what? What you want me to do 'bout that?

Eddie. I know you pissed off. You got the right. But baby, you got to think 'bout what I been goin' through.

Sue Belle/Evelina. What you been goin' through? You been sufferin', Eddie?

Eddie. It aint sufferin'. I jus' want you to know why my mind aint always workin' the way it's supposed to. Shit! I got up at four-thirty this mornin', you know that? Roosters don't even get up that early. For mo' than ten hours, I been liftin' those stink ass sheets those white folks been fuckin' all ova. And if that aint enough to make you wanta puke, them bundles weigh a ton and there aint a man workin' there, aint had his share of hernias. And them rooms are hotter'n hell . . . Sweatin' to put them mother-fuckin' bundles in those dryers . . . look at ma hands . . . All blistered and cracked . . . And that soap powder shit we use is so strong it eats away the skin and all the water in yo' hands . . . My hands so dry now if I touch paper, it sends me up the wall. I can't do nothin' with 'em . . . And them sheets come out of that dryer so hot and steamy that yo' hands go to be like asbestos to fold 'em . . .

Sue Belle. (*Unsteadily.*) Eddie . . . Eddie . . . how come you tellin' me all this?

Eddie. Because I wouldn't be there if it wasn't for you.

Sue Belle. Eddie . . .

Eddie. Befo' you, you couldn't keep me on a job like that. Shit, I couldn't think a nothin' but 'bout women and keeping cool and loose and ready to step out, baby. Anytime, you heard that Fats Domino or B.B. King or Clyde McPhatter was round, shit, you could find Eddie there steppin' out cool and loose. Now look at me? I'm bustin' ma balls out there. Tryin' to put together a few pennies. For us. Ma whole brain is tired and bleached

ACT II MY SISTER, MY SISTER 43

out. I can't think straight, you understand me. But I'm trying to hold onto this gig as long as I can, to scratch us out a start, 'cause all I want to do is take care of you. To take care of you so you wont neva be scared of nothin'. When you called me and told me about that damned singing keeping you up all night, I wanted to come ova right then and whip asses. I want to take care of you. But you got to give me time to get my head straight, and you got to know, baby, that one wrong look from you sends me climbin' the walls . . . It gets me crazy . . .

SUE BELLE. Call me baby again.

EDDIE. You know you my baby.

SUE BELLE. Am I, Eddie?

EDDIE. Anytime you want to hear it, baby. (*Crosses to hold her on daybed.*)

SUE BELLE. You my man, Eddie. I can't help lovin' you. I aint no good, but I can't help it.

EDDIE. Who in the hell said you aint no good? You my queen!

SUE BELLE. Keep tellin' me that. I need to hear it. Heah . . . Give my yo' hands . . . They been working so hard, daddy . . . Come heah . . . (*Pulling him gently and stroking his hands.*) You got such nice strong hands . . . they so big . . . Kin hold anything . . . Honey, I'm goin' to make a nice home where you wont neva want to go away. I got so much love to give you it scares me . . . If you don't use it all up, what I'm gonna do with it? If I can't have you on top of me with yo' hands rubbing me, and havin' you in me, what I'm gonna do with all them feelin's? I want to have a lotta babies and I want to love 'em and not mix 'em all up with my sayin' one thing and you saying another . . . And I want to lay in yo' arms every night and turn over and see you there askin' for me . . . I want to lay there afterwards and go to sleep and feel you all over me and in me . . . I need love, Eddie . . . the way I use to . . . But in all kinds of ways now . . .

Things are so hard to figure out now . . . You know, I can remember my Daddy would sit on the side of ma bed and jus' hold me . . . Rockin' me and singin' to me . . . Eddie, he was a lot like you . . . He was so strong with big shoulders . . . And hands like yo' hands and he was so gentle . . . And how he could laugh . . . When he wasn't there no more, there was this hole besides my bed where he used to sit . . . As if someone had jus' took scissors and cut him out the air . . .

EDDIE. Baby, look heah . . . Come on now . . . Don't get yo'self all worked up like that. We all lose somebody close to us sometime. We got to hold on to what we got left. Look here, I want you to move in wit' me . . . We got to take the chance . . . Make the break . . . You aint gonna neva be straight in this house . . . I don't like the feelin' in this place . . . (*Loud clap of thunder. A pause.*)

SUE BELLE. I think you right, Eddie.

EDDIE. You know I'm right. I neva believed in that voodoo shit befo' but this house is evil.

SUE BELLE. Oh, yeah, Eddie . . . I got to come with you but I'm jus' . . . I'm just so scared . . .

EDDIE. Well, what you scared of, baby? I'm heah.

SUE BELLE. I jus' can't up and leave. I jus' can't. I can't stop them like Evelina . . .

EDDIE. Look, Sue Belle, get yo' stuff. I mean it now. Tomorrow I'll come back and talk to yo' Mama.

SUE BELLE. What you gonna say to her?

EDDIE. I'm gonna tell her I love you and you gonna have ma baby. What you think I'm gonna say to her? (*A beat pause.*) Now get yo' stuff. (*A beat pause.*) Goddamnit, Sue Belle! What you want from yo' room? (*Rises and crosses to go upstairs.*)

SUE BELLE. No, Eddie, wait a minute!

EDDIE. What the hell for?

SUE BELLE. Oh Eddie . . . Eddie . . . In a minute, please . . . I'll get the stuff . . . But . . . but let me make you a drink first . . . jus' to relax you . . . You been working hard all day . . . (*She rises and crosses to him.*)

EDDIE. Why don't you wanta leave this house?

SUE BELLE. Eddie . . . Please . . . One drink! (*A long pause.*)

EDDIE. Alright, baby. One drink, that's it! I guess I can use it.

SUE BELLE. Good. I been hidin' it so Mama wont find it . . . (*As she is going for drink she moves upstairs to bedroom.*)

EDDIE. You heah me, Sue Belle! One drink then we goin'!

SUE BELLE/EVELINA. Yeah, Eddie . . .

EDDIE. (*Crosses and sits back in chair.*) Hey, Sue Belle . . . You know, I'm disappointed. What happened to all the religious pictures you were telling me about?

SUE BELLE/EVELINA. (*She returns.*) I took them down. You think I'm gonna let Jesus and his brothers watch us all night figuring how they gonna burn us in hell?

EDDIE. (*Laughing.*) You mean they got plans for us?

SUE BELLE/EVELINA. They gonna cook yo' ass till it's black as charcoal.

EDDIE. Can't get no blacker.

SUE BELLE/EVELINA. Everytime you fuck me, you get blacker.

EDDIE. What you mean by that?

SUE BELLE/EVELINA. (*Pouring drinks.*) I mean I love you on top of me, that's what the hell I mean; and Jesus and all his frownin' can't take that out'a ma head.

EDDIE. Well, say it, Mama!

SUE BELLE/EVELINA. Oh, shit! You don't understand me at all, do you? They gonna burn my ass till I melt like candle wax. Cause'a you. You, daddy! And you gonna burn wit' me. 'Cause you taught me how good arms are.

EDDIE. Havin' you in ma arms is worth burnin' in hell for.

SUE BELLE/EVELINA. You're fulla shit! You know that. You sho' kin talk big. You love to hold me but you neva heah when I need to be held. You kin fuck me and tell me a lotta sweet words about how everything is alright, but when you run yo' ass away, who gonna stop them voices screamin' in ma head? Not you, nigger, 'cause you aint gonna be here. (*Crosses, giving him drink and returns to kitchen chair.*)

EDDIE. There you go again with that shit. I told you I love you. What you want me to do to prove it?

SUE BELLE/EVELINA. You proved how much you loved me, nigger. You proved it already. When I tried to tell you I was pregnant, and you wouldn't lissen to nothin' but them mummies starin' and grinnin' wit' their plastic smiles, you proved it. And when you hugged me and then cut out on me jus' when I needed yo' hugs, you proved it. I couldn't stand up to Mama. You can't even stand up to her. Mama's made outa steel, and you jus' a lotta whiskey and wind . . . But you lef' me to her anyway . . . and . . . and when the time came, I couldn't go to nobody but that man with that knife stickin' into me . . . Do you know how much blood poured out'a me 'cause a you? Do you know how ma babies looked floatin' in that toilet befo' they flushed 'em away? (*A long pause.*)

EDDIE. (*Rises.*) What you talkin' 'bout? You neva told me you was gonna have a baby fer me. (*A pause.*)

SUE BELLE/EVELINA. I'm pregnant for you now, Eddie.

EDDIE. I know that . . . but I'm talkin' about this other time . . . You neva told me. Why didn't you?

SUE BELLE/EVELINA. Tell you what?

EDDIE. That you threw away my baby.

SUE BELLE/EVELINA. Yo' baby? It wasn't yo' baby.

EDDIE. What you mean?

SUE BELLE/EVELINA. It wasn't yo' baby.

EDDIE. Well . . . Well . . . Who's baby was it? (*A long pause.*)

SUE BELLE/EVELINA. That don't matter now. It's too late for that now. You . . . you had yo' chance to lissen and all you did was given sermons jus' like Mama.

EDDIE. (*Crosses and grabs her out of chair.*) I don't understand all this slick shit you givin' me. Who you been seein behind ma back?

SUE BELLE/EVELINA. Turn me aloose!

EDDIE. I asked you a question.

SUE BELLE/EVELINA. You hurtin' ma arm! Turn me aloose now!

EDDIE. Not till you give me some kinda answer!

SUE BELLE/EVELINA. What kinda answer you want? I don't have to tell you nothin'!

EDDIE. For the last two years you been fuckin' wit' ma head, and all the while slippin' behind ma back to some other man's bed, and now you tell me you don't have to tell me nothin'!

SUE BELLE/EVELINA. It's too late, Nigger! It's too late. (EDDIE *throws her hard onto daybed. A pause. He turns away. She moves to glass and bottle. She pours a glass. Quietly.*) Heah! Drink up ma liquor.

EDDIE. Sue Belle . . .

SUE BELLE/EVELINA. I said drink it! Not hold it! I got plans for yo' hands. (EDDIE *swallows it in one drink.*)

EDDIE. Is that good enough for you?

SUE BELLE/EVELINA. Not yet! (*She moves to steps, unzips and steps out of her dress.*)

EDDIE. You bitch. You don't care what you do do you? (*A pause.*) I don't know why I'm still here. (*Sits down on kitchen chair.*)

SUE BELLE/EVELINA. You'll be here until you go, Eddie . . . And then you wont neva come back. I know . . . But you'll be here until that time . . . (*Slowly she walks to the stairs, mounts two steps and sits slowly.*

Purposely she opens her legs, so that she is now a boyish figure, her thighs revealed.) Aint you sorry the way it all turned out, daddy? Aint you? I'm jus' sitting heah now 'cause aint nothin' else to do . . . Nothin' else to hold . . . You took away ma arms . . . the way you used to touch me . . . and now I'm jes' waitin' fer Mama to come down those steps at me . . . 'Cause at least when Mama whips, she hugs . . . And that's somethin' to hold onto . . . Even if it hurts when it's good . . . But you know about that . . . . Aint that what you told me that first night? . . . In that room? . . . "It hurts now but it'll be good" . . . And it was . . . good . . . Mama's strap . . . (*Voices of* MAMA *and* EVELINA [Adolescent], *offstage Left and then quickly the two enter onto upstairs landing.*)

EVELINA (Adolescent). No, Mama! No! You crazy? No!

MAMA. You ain't stayin' in this house . . . If you gonna run whorin' around, you gonna find someplace else to stay . . .

SUE BELLE/EVELINA. (*Quiet though direct.*) There ain't no other place is there, Daddy?

EVELINA (Adolescent). Who told you that lie? Who? Sue Belle did! Didn't she?!

MAMA. No, Sue Belle didn't tell me nothin'. I jus' know.

EVELINA (Adolescent). (*Running into bedroom with* MAMA *following.*) Yes, she did! I know she did!

MAMA. I ain't gonna have no whore in this house! If you want a man so bad that you gotta be jumpin' in one bed after another, you go get yo'self married.

EVELINA (Adolescent). Mama, what you gonna do with them scissors? I'm not gonna let you cut ma hair. Is that gonna make me good all of a sudden? Gonna make me a Christian? Bein' baldheaded and ugly! I ain't gonna let you do it! (*Exits out of bedroom.*)

SUE BELLE/EVELINA. Ain't it time you come yet, Daddy? Ain't it time?

MAMA. (*To* SUE BELLE [Child].) Sue Belle!!! (*Moving angrily out of bedroom, seeing* SUE BELLE [Child].) I ain't gonna have no two Evelinas in this house! One is enough! Now fix yo'self up! That's indecent the way you sittin'!

SUE BELLE (Child). Mama . . . I didn't mean nothin'.

MAMA. (*A pause.*) That sister of yours. I shouldn't be yellin' at you 'cause a the anger I got stored for her.

SUE BELLE (Child). I didn't mean nothin'.

MAMA. I know . . . Jes' straighten yo'self up . . . (*Helping her put her robe on.*)

SUE BELLE (Child). Yes, mam.

MAMA. Gimme a hug now . . . (*An overlong embrace.*) Get yo'self dressed for bed. (MAMA *exits upstairs and off Right.*)

SUE BELLE (Child). (*A long pause.*) I'm cold, Daddy . . . Ain't it time? (*Moving quickly downstairs into* EDDIE's *arms on daybed.*) Yes, Daddy . . . Yes . . . (*A long embrace as she clings.*)

EDDIE. Now what is this?!!

SUE BELLE. Make me feel good!

EDDIE. You! You! It's always you! Don't matter how Eddie feels, does it?

SUE BELLE. You ma only chance. Squeeze me in yo' arms. Make me feel right!

EDDIE. (*Her urgency is frightening now.*) Hey, baby? What is it? Hey . . .

SUE BELLE. It's so cold in heah! I can't sleep in this cold.

EDDIE. You want me to close the window. There's a draft?

SUE BELLE. No! Don't go away! Promise me you wont, Eddie. Promise me!

EDDIE. You told me to leave, goddamnit!

SUE BELLE. Can't you see I ain't responsible, Eddie? Can't you see nothin'?

EDDIE. (*A long pause and then he gathers her in.*) Alright! I'm not goin' nowhere, baby.

SUE BELLE. That's it! Hug me! Rock me! ... Big arms 'round ma neck ... Sweet black arms ... I love yo' breath .. Yo' face scratchin' mine like black sand ... Warm with the moon on yo' dark hair ... The moon meltin' into ma dream ... A hot orange ice cream scoop in your mouth ... Sweet and good ... laughin' when you kiss me ... (*She kisses him full on the mouth.*)

EDDIE. Oh, baby ... Damn what you do to me ... (*A long pause, as she pulls away. Enter* EVELINA [Adolescent] *at top of stairs.*)

EVELINA (Adolescent). Hello, Daddy ... (*A long pause.* DADDY *lifts his head slowly to* EVELINA.)

DADDY. Evelina ... (*A long pause.*) Where yo' Mama?

MAMA. (*Offstage.*) I'm in bed. How come you late?

DADDY. I ain't late. The world jus' turned the clocks fast.

MAMA. (*Offstage.*) Well, wait a minute. I'm gonna come down and warm up yo' dinner.

SUE BELLE (Child). Hello, Daddy ... (*A pause.*) I been waitin' for you ...

DADDY. Mmmmm! Mmmmm! What is this I hear? Is them bees I hear buzzin' round some sweet honey?

SUE BELLE (Child). Sho' is, Daddy!

DADDY. Watch it, little Mama, don't you sting me! Come put yo' arms round ma neck. Gimme some, some sugar! Get up on my back! (SUE BELLE [Child] *runs in* DADDY's *arms.*) Bzzzz! Bzzzz! (*Carrying* SUE BELLE [Child] *on his back around in a circle center stage.* EVELINA [Adolescent] *stands on landing.*) Hey, Evelina, what you been doin'?

EVELINA (Adolescent). I been up heah studyin' our Junior Class Play. I gotta good part in it.

DADDY. (*To* EVELINA [Adolescent] *although still nuzzling and hugging* SUE BELLE [Child].) Well, don't tell me Evelina, you gonna be a movie star. (*Loudly to* MAMA.) You hear that, Claudine. Evelina's gonna be a movie star. (*To* EVELINA [Adolescent] *as he moves around in a playful circle.*) Now you really gonna git it, Evelina. You and me gonna go straight to hell anyway to let yo' Mama tell it.

EVELINA (Adolescent). Oh heck, hell ain't so bad!

DADDY. Maybe you right! After all, Reverend Johnson ain't gonna be there is he? Shucks! Hell is gonna be a picnic.

SUE BELLE (Child). Would you fight the devil off, Daddy?

DADDY. Now whadaya think? Ain't I big enough to carry you, little Mama?

SUE BELLE (Child). Yes, suh, Daddy!

DADDY. Well, then, the devil, he ain't got a chance, is he? I'll pick him up and chuck him up against one of his hot ovens and then ... (*Dropping her back on daybed.*) ... in he'll go ... Then what we gonna have?

SUE BELLE (Child). Devil food cake!

DADDY. Mmmmm! Mmmmm! Ain't this good! You done stole all Mr. Sugarman's sugar. You sweeter than sugar!

SUE BELLE (Child). How sweet?

DADDY. So sweet that when we go to the carnival, somebody is sho' to grab yo' little bony knees and lift you up thinkin' you a candy apple ... (*Nuzzling his face into her.*)

EVELINA (Adolescent). (*A troubled laugh.*) Daddy ...

DADDY. Somebody done brung you somethin' today, sugar baby!

SUE BELLE (Child). Who done it?

DADDY. I don' know. Who done it? Who? Who? Who done it? I wanta know who done it. Tell me, Evelina, did you do it?

EVELINA (Adolescent). (*Feebly trying to join the play, still on stair landing.*) No, Daddy, I sho' didn't.

DADDY. Somebody done it . . . I wanta know who . . . And I think . . . I think it waaaaas (*To* SUE BELLE [Child].) You.

SUE BELLE (Child). Daddy! I did it! It was me! Me! Me!

DADDY. You mean you conjured up all this magic? I was jus' walkin' down the street, and I hear this little teeney voice from a sto' window callin' out to me. "Mista Earl, I heah you got a little girl who got so much sugar she don't know what to do with it all."

SUE BELLE (Child). (*Laughing.*) What else, Daddy?

DADDY. Well, I was mixed up. I sho' was. I didn't know who was talkin' to me. So I turn around and what did I see but this big fat blubber fat lady walkin' in backa me . . . Jus' walkin' . . . Oooooooh Lord, she was movin' out in all directions . . . Jus' walking . . . And I said, "Oh, no, by God! That can't be her talkin'! She look like she already done stole all the sugar and already done filled up what ain't even pockets." So I jus' stepped aside and said, "Walk on by, fat lady . . . Jus' walk on by . . ."

SUE BELLE (Child). How she walk, Daddy?

DADDY. Like this! (*Walking wobbily legged.*) Like she was floatin' in a blowed-up inner tube without no water. So anyway this little voice calls out again, "Take me home, Mister Earl, where I kin get some sugar. I'm little and I need a lotta love to grow up to be strong." And I looked, and there she was . . . not bigger'n my hand . . . Jus' winkin' at me . . . She just flirtin' with me . . . Oooooh she was fresh! I said, "Come on heah, sweet thing . . . You jes' come on . . . jump on in ma lunch bag heah." And she did . . . And heah she is . . . (*Takes* PETAL *out of bag.*)

SUE BELLE (Child). Daddy! Daddy! She cute! She so cute! What's her name?

DADDY. Well, ask her.

SUE BELLE (Child). What's yo' name, little baby?
DADDY. (*Falsetto voice.*) "My name is Petal. What's yo' name?"
SUE BELLE (Child). I'm yo' new Mama Sue Belle. Come on. I wanta show you yo' soul sisters and soul brothers. (*Rises and crosses upstairs to landing.*)
EVELINA (Adolescent). Tch! Oh God! (*Crossing downstairs to her* DADDY.)
SUE BELLE (Child). Hey, Daddy, guess what? Dolly gonna get married. (*Crosses into bedroom.*)
EVELINA (Adolescent). Daddy . . .
DADDY. Well, hush ma mouth! I sho' hope she don't come up heah wit' no babies too quick! We already done got fifteen! (*Winking at* EVELINA [Adolescent]).
EVELINA (Adolescent). Daddy, I wanta talk to you.
DADDY. 'Bout what?
SUE BELLE (Child). (*Comes out of bedroom to landing and returns to* D. R.) Come on, Daddy, we gotta find some place for Petal to sleep.
DADDY. Yes, we do. (*As a second thought to* EVELINA [Adolescent]). In a minute, Evelina. (*Starts up the stairs. A brief pause, then comes back down to* EVELINA.) You studyin' hard on yo' play?
EVELINA (Adolescent). Oh, Daddy . . .
DADDY. Well, what you lookin' so sour for? Ain't you enjoyin' it?
EVELINA (Adolescent). Yes, suh . . .
DADDY. What part you playin'?
EVELINA (Adolescent). I'm playin' a real rich lady but I can't talk too proper.
DADDY. Well, tell yo' Mama to get Miss Beatrice ova heah and you jus' lissen good to her phony talk. That's one white woman sho' kin talk proper. "Gooood evenin', Evelina."
EVELINA (Adolescent). Don't make me laugh, Daddy.
DADDY. Well, what's wrong with a little bit of laughin'? (*Moves upstairs into bedroom.*)

EVELINA (Adolescent). But not now, Daddy! (*Follows her* DADDY *as far as doorway.*)

SUE BELLE (Child). (*Mimicing bass voice.*) "Hello, Petal, dey call me Crazy Ed. How is you?"

DADDY. (*Mimicing falsetto.*) "I's fine, and you, suh?"

SUE BELLE (Child). "We sho' is glad to have you in da fam'ly."

DADDY. "Thank you, Mr. Crazy Ed, that's real nice of you to say so. Tee! Hee! Hee!" (*He moves over to bed with* SUE BELLE.)

EVELINA (Adolescent). Daddy!

SUE BELLE (Child). Daddy, I don't think Dolly likes Petal.

DADDY. Dolly, you stop bein' so selfish. You can't have all the men.

SUE BELLE (Child). Oh, Daddy, I love her! Petal is so cute!

DADDY. Pay the sugarman his sugar!

EVELINA (Adolescent). (*Cold, quiet, monotone.*) Las' month, I skipped school and went to the rockpit all day . . . Rufus was there and Cliff and John and Lionel . . . We was all swimming . . . I was the only girl there . . . they didn't want me there at first but I wanted to be there . . .

DADDY. Come on, let Daddy carry his sweet Mama to bed!

EVELINA (Adolescent). There was a lotta trees . . . Couldn't see the road or houses or nothin' . . . And then they was glad I came . . . One at a time . . . They was glad . . . You ever listen to me, Daddy?

DADDY. What, Evelina, honey? What?

EVELINA (Adolescent). Daddy, them dolls ain't real?

DADDY. Evelina, what you yellin' 'bout?

EVELINA (Adolescent). One after another they come in heah . . . I'm sick'a playin' shadow to them things.

DADDY. Whaaaat? Evelina, don't tell me you jealous of yo' little sista?

EVELINA (Adolescent). It's mo' than that, Daddy!

DADDY. Come here! Come here! (*Hugging* EVELINA [Adolescent]. *Sits on bed and sits* EVELINA *on his knee.*) You too big to be cryin' fer nothin', Evelina . . .

EVELINA (Adolescent). I'm fifteen years old, Daddy. I ain't too big for nothin' . . .

SUE BELLE (Child). Daddy, I like when you walk . . . You big shoes sound like thunder . . . Walk real loud for me when you go downstairs . . .

DADDY. (*Holding out his arms for* SUE BELLE [Child]. *She crawls under his other arm.*) Come ovah heah, little Mama . . .

EVELINA [Adolescent]. How come I can't neva talk to you, Daddy, without Sue Belle climbin' all in it?

DADDY. Evelina, Sue Belle ain't nothin' but a child.

EVELINA (Adolescent). I know that.

DADDY. Yo' daddy's got enough arms heah to hold both his girls. Evelina, you gotta know I love both my girls. Don't you be gettin' evil round heah. You old enough to know that you see what you lookin' for, sugar . . . And if you blind, you can't see nothin'. (*A pause.*) You get yo'self ready fer bed . . . I'll go down and say hello to yo' Mama then I'll come back . . . You and me, Evelina, we'll have a talk . . . Jus' ourselves . . .

SUE BELLE (Child). Walk like thunder, Daddy . . .

DADDY. (*Laughing and pulling* SUE BELLE [Child's] *hair.*) "Long plaits, comb and pick . . . On yo' shoulders like lickery sticks!" (*He exits from bedroom, walks down the steps halfway, stops. He is deeply disturbed. Gets bottle and glass from kitchen table and goes and sits in chair stage Left.*)

EVELINA (Adolescent). Talk . . . Talk . . . Always talk . . . And laughin' . . . He really thinks he likes me . . . He don't even know his own feelin's . . . (*A pause.*) I hope it's a fat ugly water-head baby. (SUE BELLE *lays down on bed and* EVELINA *sits on the side of bed as lights fade to a lower register.* DADDY *continues down stairs. He picks up bottle, drinking down*

a huge swallow and then another and then a third.
MAMA *enters from upstage door Left, moves down stairs.* DADDY *sits on the chair stage Left.*)

MAMA. Earl . . .

DADDY. (*Absently.*) Hello, Claudine . . .

MAMA. How was yo' day? (*A long pause.*) Earl?

DADDY. What you say, Claudine?

MAMA. How was yo' day?

DADDY. My day? My day? I'd jes' like to put ma head back and laugh and laugh till the roof tears open! (*A long pause. She moves from kitchen stove and sits in kitchen chair stage Right.*)

MAMA. Yo' food's warmin' up. (*A long pause;* EVELINA *sits staring.*)

SUE BELLE (Child). Evelina, you mad at me?

EVELINA (Adolescent). Leave me alone, Sue Belle.

SUE BELLE (Child). Don't you wanna get dressed fer bed.

EVELINA (Adolescent). I'm gonna get out this crazy house. Daddy playin' Amos and Andy every night. Mama pushin' her Jesus! Gonna make me a Christian by choppin' off ma hair. How that gonna straighten me up? All it's gonna do is make me ugly and bulldikish . . . No boy won't neva look ma way . . . Well, I ain't gonna let that happen. I'm gonna let ma hair grow long . . . I'm gonna buy me curlers and a straighten comb . . . I'm gonna do ma hair up right . . . Burn it till it's straight and shinin' like silk . . .

SUE BELLE (Child). How come you gonna do that?

EVELINA (Adolescent). I wanna do it.

SUE BELLE (Child). Won't you burn yo' head?

EVELINA (Adolescent). It's worth it. You think you look pretty with that nappy hair of yours?

SUE BELLE. (Child). I don' care if I don't look pretty.

EVELINA (Adolescent). You wouldn't. Oh, no! Not you!

SUE BELLE (Child). Evelina, how come you make

Mama so mad at you all the time? You don't have to. How come you don't neva come home befo' dark?

EVELINA (Adolescent). You so good. Jus' wait till some man gets a wholea you. I wanna be here when they do. I want to see it.

SUE BELLE (Child). You hate me 'cause Daddy likes me, don't you? (EVELINA *glares at her. After a long silence*, EVELINA *stands, walks to the window sill and with two great sweeps pushes the dolls out the window.* SUE BELLE *screaming and moving from foot of bed to the window.*) Evelina, stop it . . . You killin' 'em . . . Stop . . . Oh ma God . . .

EVELINA (Adolescent). Shut up!!!

SUE BELLE (Child). You killin' ma babies!!!

EVELINA. (Adolescent). Didn't I tell you to shet up? (*She swings out, punching* SUE BELLE [Child] *in the stomach.*) Didn't I? (*She hits her again.*) Well why don't you cry out for Mama? (*She hits her again.*) Cry! (*And again.*) Cry!!! Cry!!!

SUE BELLE (Child). I ain't gonna cry! Mama'll come in heah and whip you like the las' time! You already hate me now!

EVELINA (Adolescent). You ain't human. You can't even cry when you hurt. (*A long pause;* EVELINA *sits staring at* SUE BELLE *who has sunk on the bed clutching her stomach, whimpering for breath.*) Shoulda thrown them things out a long time ago. (*A pause.*) Well, ain't you gonna run downstairs to see if maybe they broke their arms or their necks or somethin'?

SUE BELLE (Child). (*Whimpering, struggling to catch her breath.*) I . . . I . . . Mmmm . . . Ooh . . .

EVELINA (Adolescent). What kinda Mama are you? Layin' there like that and yo' babies cryin' fer you?

SUE BELLE (Child). I'll . . . I'll get 'em . . . later . . . I'll . . .

EVELINA (Adolescent). Later? I thought you loved them so much. You sit around feedin' 'em and dressin' 'em? You jus' gonna let 'em sit down there and suffer?

SUE BELLE (Child). Mama . . . Mama might get m-mad at you . . . Oooh . . .

EVELINA (Adolescent). Well . . . I thought so . . . You jus' like Daddy . . . You're a phoney . . . You know they ain't real, don't you . . . Don't you . . . (*Pulling her again. A long pause, as* SUE BELLE [Child] *struggles to contain the tears and pain.*) Why don't you sit up straight?

SUE BELLE (Child). I can't. It hurts.

EVELINA (Adolescent). You want me to call Mama?

SUE BELLE (Child). No.

EVELINA (Adolescent). Well, stop bendin' over like that.

SUE BELLE (Child). I hurt, Evelina. (EVELINA *watches her.*)

EVELINA (Adolescent). Sue Belle . . . Sue Belle . . . (*Tentatively, she moves to her and kneels down beside her.*) Sue Belle, sit up . . . (*She lifts* SUE BELLE [Child], *by shoulders.*) Come on now . . . I'm sorry I hit you . . . I am . . . I'll go get yo' babies fer you . . . Come on now, Sue Belle . . . Stop cryin' . . .

SUE BELLE (Child). You ain't always mean like this, Evelina. I don't like it when you act mean.

EVELINA (Adolescent). I know it . . . Oh shit! . . . Daddy! . . . That son of a bitch! . . . No good drunk! . . . Always havin' to be brought home, dumpin' him in that chair . . . Him pukin' all ova hisself . . .

SUE BELLE (Child). (*Fighting for her daddy.*) Evelina, how come . . . how come . . . that's our Daddy . . .

EVELINA (Adolescent). That nigger ain't ma daddy! . . . Stinkin' up the house . . . A no-good wino! . . . Ain't you never smelled the whiskey on his breath!

SUE BELLE (Child). (*Fighting for her daddy.*) I don't care if he do drink. I love him.

EVELINA. (Adolescent). (*A pause—a terrible calm.*)

Yeah, you do. You love yo' daddy. (*A pause. She returns to* SUE BELLE *on bed and sits.*) Sue Belle . . .

SUE BELLE (Child). Leave me alone.

EVELINA (Adolescent). (*A terrible calm.*) Come heah. Come heah a minute.

SUE BELLE (Child). I don't wanna talk no mo'.

EVELINA (Adolescent). You my little sister, ain't you?

SUE BELLE (Child). Yeah.

EVELINA (Adolescent). And you wanta be ma soul sister, right?

SUE BELLE (Child). I don't know . . . I . . . I think so . . .

EVELINA (Adolescent). Well, if you wanta be like me, you gotta learn things? Don't you, sista?

SUE BELLE (Child). Yeah . . . I guess so . . .

EVELINA (Adolescent). Well, you know how you like babies so much? You wanna know how babies come? How they really come? I got one growing in me . . .

SUE BELLE (Child). Growin' in you? What you mean?

EVELINA (Adolescent). (*Pointed and cruel; slow, methodical.*) Jus' what I said . . . The baby is in ma stomach and pretty soon he gonna come out ma pussy in a lotta blood and pus . . .

SUE BELLE (Child). They don't!

EVELINA (Adolescent). It's true. A man lays on top of you, puts his dick between yo' legs, right in yo' pussy . . . And he moves . . .

SUE BELLE (Child). I don't wanna hear about it. That's ugly! (EVELINA *shakes her.*)

EVELINA (Adolescent). Now you jus' be quiet and sit still. You like babies soooo much . . . You gonna learn somethin' now . . . (EVELINA [Adolescent] *leans into* SUE BELLE [Child], *talking in hushed tones as the lights fade to about half the register and comes back up in kitchen-living room.*)

MAMA. You ready for yo' dinner? (*Rises and crosses to stove.*)

DADDY. No. Sit down. Sit down.

MAMA. Yo' food is hot.

DADDY. It kin wait a bit.

MAMA. Alright, if that's what you want. (*A pause.*) You been drinkin'? (*She sits at kitchen table.*)

DADDY. Stopped off at the bar. Had three or four sittin' heah. (*Pause.*) How come you go to bed so early? You sick?

MAMA. I been havin' dizzy spells and this numbness in ma arms all day . . . Mus' be comin' down with a cold or somethin' . . .

DADDY. I was jus' upstairs talkin' to Evelina . . . That girl's got a lotta deep meanness stirrin' 'round in her . . .

MAMA. I know . . . I can't say nothin' to her no more. I think maybe if you didn't drink so much . . . Well . . . Especially 'round the house . . .

DADDY. Is that it, you think . . .

MAMA. I don't know . . . Evelina's so bullheaded. She needs limits . . .

DADDY. I don't know . . . I jus' don't know . . . (SUE BELLE, *clutching her stomach, struggling to keep her wretching silent, sinks onto landing.*) I ain't lucky enough to have the answers. (*A pause.*) Claudine, you remember a long time back how we used to sit around talking 'bout the family we was gonna have? Neva had that boy . . . But that's no neva mind . . . Them two girls we got was the loveliest things eva to come into my life . . . Didn't I love to come home to their kisses . . . Ah, yeah . . . You used to laugh a lot then, Claudine . . . Yo fat cheeks was like two ripe cherries . . . You was some good lookin' brown woman . . . My! My! . . . We used to laugh a lot then . . .

MAMA. We spent a lotta time in juke joints, Earl . . . Every other night almost . . . Drinkin' alot and swearin' . . . That's how I remember it . . . Things

ACT II   MY SISTER, MY SISTER   61

had to change when the children came . . . Sue Belle was jus' born . . . Evelina was close to nine befo' we got sense . . . You know we used to leave her wit' our folks more'n she was with us . . . Thank God, we got sense. That night I remember I was jus' sittin', drinkin' my rum, watchin' you roarin' and cussin' from table to table . . . And them pains in ma head started from nowhere . . . And I couldn't go back in them places no more . . .

DADDY. But ain't you ever sorry about them times, Claudine? I don't mean leavin' the children like we did. But the closeness and the laughing . . . Don't you ever miss that? (*A pause.*) But of course, you don't. (*A pause.*) Too many strangers livin' wit' us . . . Can't say a word without them comin' out our mouths. Damn! If we coulda just changed without them strangers movin' in, things would be fine . . .

MAMA. Earl, I don't understand what you sayin'. (SUE BELLE's *silent wretching has stopped now; she leans forward, still sick but listening now.*)

DADDY. Well, it ain't an easy thing to see, Claudine. 'Cause things ain't always one way or the other. You see I know we was young and foolish and was wrong with our runnin' around like we did, but that don't make it all wrong. But 'cause them things is with us now, them strangers . . . we ain't thinkin', and what we did wrong in the old days makes even the right in them times wrong . . . 'Cause we ain't judgin' no mo' . . . Oh, no, they don't come in yo' do. At least in the flesh! No suh! Ma ole man used to say all the time, if you gonna keep yo' family healthy and together, you got to keep yo' do' slammed good and tight against the world. March round yo' property with a shotgun if you got to. I used to laugh at him. I figgered he was jes' an ole man bitter with livin' . . . But that ole man was wise. Let the world come in and they're judgin' . . . tellin' you what to think . . . Always judgin' . . . And it's always this or that . . . Neva a little of each

... And they don't neva leave once they in yo' head ...

MAMA. I'll take up yo' food, Earl.

DADDY. I don't eat on no schedule!

MAMA. You got the devil in you tonight, don't you?

DADDY. Ain't it the truth? And he don't tell me what not to do. He leaves me be. With the ole devil, I don't have to do nothin' but die and stay black ... I used to watch my ole man stumblin' around, talkin' out his head ... "Not me," I said. "I ain't gonna neva be that weak." Now ain't that somethin'! Funny how things can turn around. Run so hard from what's inside you, you get tired quick and it catches you. Then you know. Sanctimonious people are like that! It's always them .... them ... them ... They got the right answers. Ain't no time to feel a little bit for the people they figger is wrong. They got all the answers. Till it happens to them, too.

MAMA. You're drunk!

DADDY. You hear anything of what I jus' said?

MAMA. I hear you. You gettin' drunk again. There's children in this house, Earl. But I guess you don't care 'bout that.

DADDY. What did I say that the children can't hear?

MAMA. It's impossible to talk to you when you drinkin' ... So you jes' do what you want ... Jes' suit yo'self, Earl ...

DADDY. (*Rises center stage.*) And that finishes that, don't it? "Suit yo'self!" You got all the answers. You know all the secrets! You automatically right and anybody who questions you just a bit gotta be patted on the head and jus' humoured and jus' "Suit yo'self!" You and yo' holly roller shit! Dunk me in some water and I'm saved! Slice off ma hair and I radiate goodness. Gonna climb up to glory! Shakin' ma finger at all you drunk sinners! Gonna burn in hell! Well, give me a drunk anytime! At least, they feel! They ain't perfect, I know. But they don't threaten a person with horrible sufferin', if he don't believe in drinkin', too. No suh! There's somethin' wrong with yo' kind of people who got to be dressin' up with weird clothes to let people know you religious. Always spoutin' off at the mouth 'bout burnin' in hell and sufferin' to go to heaven 'cause you scared to get out there and try a little bi of livin' . . . Yeah, and hurtin' . . . And makin' mistakes, too . . . Them robes and shit you wear is like a cage . . . Look, look at the good people . . . Don't come in our cage and we won't come out . . . And don't touch . . . No suh . . .

MAMA. If you don't have sense enough to listen to the truth when you hear it, Earl, I'm just sorry for you! (EVELINA *kneels behind* SUE BELLE, *pulling her head up to whisper.*)

DADDY. Whose truth? It ain't mine!

MAMA. Everything I believe in is in the Bible!

DADDY. The Bible is a book! It ain't alive! It don't live in this house! And there ain't no chance in hell that you can live the pages from a book, I don't care how right you say it is. It don't live! Where is the little bit a closeness we had when we was young? And don't tell me 'bout headaches and drinkin'. At least we made them mistakes together! Now, I don't know where you live. You jus' a real safe, cold, clean book for Jesus. You sho' ain't no woman. Where is yo' mouth I used to kiss? I wanta fina that page. Where is the legs that took in ma babies? You nailed 'em up on a neon cross wit' yo' Jesus and now you tryin' to get . . .

SUE BELLE (Child). It ain't true! It ain't! It ain't! (*Moves quickly out of bedroom and sits on stairs with* EVELINA *following.*)

MAMA. (*Rises.*) Sue Belle! What you doin' up there?

SUE BELLE (Child). Mama . . . Mama . . . Please, tell Evelina to hush . . .

EVELINA (Adolescent). Yeah! Tell me to hush, Mama.

MAMA. I told you to go to bed, Evelina! Sue Belle!

SUE BELLE (Child). (*Crosses to stairs.*) I don't feel good, Mama.

MAMA. I don't know what's goin' on up there but I mean fer both a you to quit! You hear me, Evelina! Take Sue Belle back to bed!

EVELINA (Adolescent). I wanta talk to ma Daddy.

DADDY. Evelina, me and yo' Mama talkin'! Now go in yo' room like you been told.

MAMA. What for? You been talkin' loud enough they kin heah you in the next block.

DADDY. Well, I talk loud 'cause I do everything loud, Claudine! I laugh loud! I love loud! I even cry loud, Claudine, 'cause that's what happens when you're reachin' for somebody who ain't livin'.

MAMA. I ain't gonna lissen to you, Earl. (*She moves up the stairs.*) Come on, get up, Sue Belle . . .

DADDY. Oh, goddamnit, yes you will listen. You gonna heah, Claudine. This is gonna be the las' night that I let this roof smother me woman. And if I scream out against what you let in heah to take over ma house and ma children, I'm gonna make sho' you heah that scream. You heah me.

MAMA. I hear you, Earl . . . And I think that's best . . . By all means, don't let this roof smother you another night.

DADDY. (*A pause, quieter.*) You think I'm jes' down on yo' religion, Claudine . . . That ain't where I'm comin' from . . . Wether I believe in yo' Jesus or not, which I don't . . .

MAMA. I know you don't!

DADDY. That ain't got nothin' to do with it! No, Claudine, it don't! 'Cause it's got to be the devil hisself you worshippin' and if that ain't the case, you buildin' this Jesus of yours into some kind of White Bossman cracking his whip ova all us Colored people . . . Oh I here you every night tellin' these children about Black sin, about Satan comin' from some Black pit, about Black evil this and Black evil that . . . Well, don't yo'

Jesus give you eyes? Ain't you neva looked at me? At yo'self? At yo' children? We all Black! We don't stand a chance wit' yo' kinda Jesus! We don't stand a chance! It would be better if you just broke them children all up so they'd be crippled. Somehow they could mend through all that . . . But you're tearin' up their minds, and when that's gone, what and who is gonna help 'em? How they gonna love when they look in the mirror and everything laughin' back at them is evil? (*A pause.*)

EVELINA (Adolescent). Daddy?

DADDY. What, Evelina?

EVELINA (Adolescent). You finish talkin' and talkin' and talkin', Daddy?

DADDY. What you say, Evelina?

EVELINA (Adolescent). You said you was gonna come right back to talk to me . . . Sooon as you said hello to Mama . . .

DADDY. Evelina, I told you one time already. Go in yo' room and don't let me tell you no mo'.

EVELINA (Adolescent). But Daddy, you told me . . .

SUE BELLE (Child). Mama, I feel real sick.

EVELINA (Adolescent). Oh shet up, you simple-minded little bitch!

MAMA. What did you say, Evelina?

EVELINA (Adolescent). What did I say?!!! Oh, now you want to hear that! Well, I said cocksucker, whore, slut, bitch, cunt, mother-fucker . . . (MAMA *charging upstairs at her.*) You ain't gonna hit me! You betta not hit me!

DADDY. (*Also moving upstairs at her now.*) Evelina, shut yo' mouth.

EVELINA (Adolescent). I won't shet ma mouth. I gotta right to talk as much as you! I ain't dead! I ain't a part a these walls!

DADDY. (*Grabbing her by her shoulders and shaking her fiercely.*) Shut up! Shut up!

SUE BELLE (Child). Daddy, you hurtin' her!

MAMA. That's enough, Earl!

SUE BELLE (Child). She don't mean nothin', Daddy! She jes' wanna talk! Daddy! Turn ma sister loose!!! (DADDY *releases her and throws her on bed.*) Evelina . . .

EVELINA (Adolescent). (*A long pause and then to* DADDY.) It's too bad ain't it, Daddy? I ain't big enough to bully nobody into listenin' to me. But you don't have to worry 'bout me no mo'. Shadows don't cry . . . turn out the light; they jes' go away . . . (DADDY *slowly crosses out of bedroom and downstairs over to day bed, Center.* SUE BELLE *moves towards* EVELINA *but she lifts her head and glares at her.* SUE BELLE *stops without touching her.* SUE BELLE *walks slowly out of the bedroom to landing. A beat pause or two later,* MAMA *moves over to* EVELINA.)

SUE BELLE (Child). (*After a long pause, accusing, sharing sister's pain.*) Evelina . . . Evelina . . . You hurt her, Daddy . . . You hurt her bad . . . (*A pause.*) This house too cold . . . I'm scared, Daddy . . . (*She crosses to daybed and* DADDY *holds her. Frightened by her brief rejection of her father.*) I love yo' kisses . . . When you laugh . . . I love yo' breath . . . When you walk like thunder . . . (*A pause.*) Jesus . . . Jesus . . . (*Exit* EVELINA [Adolescent] *and* MAMA *from bedroom upstage door.*)

SUE BELLE. Ain't nothin' heah . . . Nobody heah . . . Nothin' to hold on to . . . Nothin' but them . . . And that . . . the roof . . . rotten wood . . . crackin' . . . lettin' in the rain . . . fallin' on me . . . Sufferin' . . . Seein' heaven . . . Ain't no blue up there . . . Rain leakin' in . . . Can't catch heaven in a basin . . . don't come in now . . . Only water-head babies . . .

SUE BELLE/EVELINA. Talk some magic, Daddy . . . Bring 'em back . . . Can't . . . they drowned . . . Stained red . . . Washed out from between ma legs into that White man's long hairy fingers diggin' into me . . . Lost 'em to the toilet . . . they was floatin' there . . . sof' pieces of clay . . . Somebody just be-

ginnin' to press in ma babies' arms and legs and face
. . . drowned in all that blood . . . Neva figured they'd
come from Jesus . . . Hard cold faces . . . Hair like
ropes . . . Sittin' on the window sill . . . can't cry
. . . can't suffer . . . lies . . . 'Cause Mama said it
was dirty . . . Only Black people do that . . . No
good people . . . You on top'a me . . . Feelin' so good
. . . It felt so good . . . Didn't want it to stop . . .
It hurt and it felt good . . .

EDDIE. Sue Belle, don't jes' sit there starin' like that
. . . Come on, you're scarin' me, come on . . .

SUE BELLE/EVELINA. (*A long pause as she lifts head
to stare at* EDDIE.) You? You? Scared, Eddie? Oh, that's
funny. That's really funny. (*Laughing now.*) You supposed to protect me. Ain't that somethin'! I bragged
'bout you. I told 'em you was comin' to help me. That
really mean I ain't got a chance now. (*A pause.*) You
ain't got what I need. You jes' like me. You runnin',
too. 'Cause if you take away the lies, there ain't no
magic in livin' good. Might as well be a bitch dog
fuckin' in the heat . . . That's all . . . That's all you
got to offer me . . . But I don't need that . . . I don't
need no nigger humpin' on top'a me . . . I want a little
bita magic . . . Give me that, Eddie . . .

EDDIE. Ain't it too bad you ain't White!

SUE BELLE/EVELINA. Ain't it tho'? 'Cause I know
'bout White men. I had one up heah, too . . . Right in
that bedroom . . . With all yo' broken-up babies lookin'
on . . . And afterwards he had ma sista . . . 'Cause
she wanted it . . . All the while . . . Now, you see
why I picked you. 'Cause I ain't neva been worth nothin'.

EDDIE. Sue Belle, I know you ain't right. I know that.
But you don't need me, baby. I'm gonna give you all
the space you need fer all the White men you seem to
want so much . . .

SUE BELLE/EVELINA. Is it that time, Eddie . . . Is
it that time?

EDDIE. Yeah. It's that time. I don't know what took me so long.

SUE BELLE/EVELINA. Jus' close the do' behind you, Daddy. (EDDIE *moves to button his shirt, to slip into his jacket and his raincoat.* SPECTRES *enter slowly to the edges of the house, waiting and watching, the funeral wreaths poised again, sheets ceremoniously draped across outstretched arms.*) Close it tight on yo' face. And don't think I'll waste one second lookin' at you. I might think 'bout you; I can't help that. But I won't remember yo' face. I'll remember the Whiskey on yo' breath . . . I walk the streets where they call me a whore and I'll feel you in the air . . . But I won't remember yo' face. I'll fill up that empty space with somebody else . . . somebody else . . . or somethin' . . . Stupid . . . Stupid little bitch . . . When it's rainin', walkin' the street . . . Sittin' by herself . . . Watchin' every Colored man who walks by hopin' it's Daddy . . . And my sister, she can't even remember how he looks . . .

EDDIE. You can't even hold a lie straight, can you?

SUE BELLE/EVELINA. What am I lyin' 'bout?

EDDIE. You told me yo' sista was dead.

SUE BELLE/EVELINA. I told you she was sick.

EDDIE. You'd lie on yo' grave. (*She stoops, fumbling under the couch, pulling out the pictures, seeing the* SPECTRES, *becoming more anxious now.*)

SUE BELLE/EVELINA. (*She hands him that child-like drawing.*) Heah, Eddie . . . Look at it . . .

EDDIE. What is it?

SUE BELLE/EVELINA. A picture of Jesus . . . My sista drew it . . .

EDDIE. Yo' sista drew this . . . It's like somethin' a little kid would draw . . . You told me yo' sista was grown . . .

SUE BELLE/EVELINA. (*A beat pause.*) Did I, Eddie?

EDDIE. What's wrong witchu? You know you did. You was lookin' for her that night I met you. And that was two years ago . . . Look at it . . . This thing was drawn a long time ago . . . Look how it's all fading down . . .

SUE BELLE/EVELINA. (*Taking the picture from him.*) It is fading out . . .

SUE BELLE. (*She leans back into him.*) Eddie . . . Eddie . . . you remember that first night I saw you in front of the Knightbeat?

EDDIE. Yeah . . . I shoulda known that night I was in trouble . . . the way you turned me on, I shoulda known, my mind was gonna be messed up . . . I wanted you so goddamned bad, I don't know what I woulda done if you had said no.

SUE BELLE. I woulda said no too, Eddie . . . But it felt so good . . . you touchin' me . . .

EDDIE. You was somethin'; you was a beautiful little bitch . . . My God! Walkin' by the Knightbeat in them tight blue jeans . . . yo' little ass jus' a handful . . . God! You was walkin' wit' yo' head down, not seein' nobody . . . Like you didn't have nobody nowhere . . . Hell, you never even took a drink befo' that night.

SUE BELLE. (*A faint smile as she remembers.*) I was so scared . . . I really was . . . I had neva been down that part a town so late . . .

EDDIE. Did you see me right away?

SUE BELLE. You was leaning on the side of the building with yo' friends jivin' round with the girls as they walked by . . . You had a green cap on and shades on yo' eyes and you smiled at me . . .

EDDIE. What did you think when you saw me? You dig me right away?

SUE BELLE. (*Laughing.*) Ain't you somethin'?

EDDIE. Well, did you?

SUE BELLE. I stopped didn't I?

EDDIE. You knew a good thing when you saw it.

SUE BELLE. (*Laughing.*) Yeah . . . But I was scared . . . Oooo man . . . When you took me up in that motel room, I couldn't breathe . . .

EDDIE. Well, you wasn't the only one scared.

SUE BELLE. You sho' didn't act like you was scared.

EDDIE. You was fourteen years old, baby. I had neva been wit' no girl that young. If you asked me straight out, I woulda let you go. Did you know that? But you kept starin' at me, lookin' up at me, sayin', "Have you seen my sista? I'm lookin' for my sista" . . . Ova and ova . . . I tried to get from yo' eyes but I swear you wouldn't let me move . . . All them lies about lookin' for some sista . . . (SPECTRES *begin to move in now, the sheets being draped and covering the kitchen table, the large chair at left and the daybed, the wreaths are once again being placed* D. R. *of daybed.*)

SUE BELLE. That wasn't no lie. . . . I wish it was. . . . (*A pause as she walks around looking at* MAMA *and the* SPECTRES.) I wish it was, Mama. . . . I wish you didn't come back from Jacksonville that night. . . . You was worried 'cause I was sick. And you walked in that room and found me and Evelina and that man. . . . Mama just sat on that couch and she neva moved no mo' . . . Reverend Johnson wouldn't let the doctor come. . . . They jus' sang and sang and sang. . . . Ma sista neva came to the funeral. . . . (*Turning to* EDDIE *again.*) Ma sista ran out the house so fast; she was bleedin' from Mama's strap. . . . Ain't neva seen her no mo'. . . . I came out every night lookin' for her. . . . Fer two years. . . . But I was lookin' for you too, Eddie. . . . I guess. . . . But it didn't make no difference. . . .

EDDIE. Sue Belle?

SUE BELLE. Yes, Eddie.

EDDIE. You comin' out this house with me. I ain't takin' no for an answer. You ain't got no cause to be heah. I don't understand it all what you sayin'; I don't know if I can; I ain't as smart as a lotta people.

SUE BELLE. You beautiful, Eddie.

EDDIE. I want you to come home wit' me now . . . You won't be sorry . . . Things gonna be fine . . .

SUE BELLE. You know what's so sad, Eddie . . . I was so careful to make sho' it smiled at me . . . But it still faded away . . . it still did . . .

EDDIE. Sue Bell, you comin' wit' me, ain't you, baby? We gonna make our own home.

EVELINA (Adult). (*Taped.*) Sue Belle . . . (*Enter* MAMA. *She's dressed in robe and headdress the same as* SPECTRES *now. She sits on the daybed, staring out.* (SPECTRES *begin their singing now of "Come by Here, Lord," slowly, hauntingly.*)

SUE BELLE. (*Quietly resigned; she answers voice.*) Yes, Evelina.

EVELINA. (Adult.) (*Taped.*) What time is Mama comin' home?

SUE BELLE. Mama is in Jacksonville.

EVELINA (Adult). (*Taped.*) Did she take her robe?

SUE BELLE. She ironed it befo' she left and put it in a shopping bag . . .

EDDIE. Sue Belle, you comin' wit' me, ain't you? (SUE BELLE *walks to him, kisses him lightly.*)

SUE BELLE. I'm gonna come . . . But you go on . . . You go on ahead . . . Then I'll follow you . . . Okay? . . . Um, I'll find you . . . I jus' wanta close up . . . Ain't no rush . . . Go on now . . . Don't worry . . . Tomorrow morning come for me early . . . Alright? . . . I'll be heah . . . Go on . . . Don't worry . . .

EDDIE. Well, I got to get the place straight . . . It's really a mess . . .

SUE BELLE. You do that, honey . . . that sounds real nice . . . You come back for me . . . I'll see you . . . Alright?

EDDIE. Alright, baby . . . Comin' back heah at six o'clock . . . You gonna be ready . . .

SUE BELLE. Yeah . . . I'm gonna be ready . . . (*Exit* EDDIE. SUE BELLE *walks to the center of the room and turns to the door waiting. Enter* EVELINA [Adult].)

EVELINA (Adult). (*To unseen figure.*) Come on, stupid. Mama ain't home. (*Enter White* MAN *nervously. For the first time,* MAMA *turns head and looks at* SUE BELLE. *Her gaze follows* SUE BELLE *through the balance of the scene.*)

EVELINA (Adult). That's ma sista. Little sweet thing, ain't she? Loves herself anything White. Brought someone home to meet you, Sue Belle . . . Sho' you'll like it . . . (SUE BELLE *stands quietly, resigned. The* MAN *walks to her.*)

MAN. Hi. Yo' sista told me about you. My, you're really a sweet little thing, ain't you, honey? (*He reaches out tentatively and touches her breasts. She does not resist. She does not move. Boldly now, he moves closer, sliding his hand inside her robe caressing her breast, then her thighs.*) You colored girls are sho' built nice.

EVELINA (Adult). Well, Sue Belle? Well? Mama ain't home now . . . Come on upstairs wit' me and the man . . . Ain't gonna be no problem . . . Come on . . . (EVELINA *takes one of her hands; the* MAN *takes the other.* SUE BELLE *does not resist as they lead her towards the stairs. Simultaneously, two* SPECTRES *move in toward* MAMA; *as before, one prays over* MAMA *while the other fans her. The picture of the death and funeral has locked into* SUE BELLE's *guilt again.* SUE BELLE *stops at the top of the stairs and turns to her* MAMA.)

SUE BELLE. (*Quietly.*) Sorry, Mama . . . (MAMA *turns her head front closing her eyes.* SUE BELLE *turns and walks into the bedroom with* EVELINA *and the* MAN *following her.*)

BLACKOUT

MY SISTER, MY SISTER SOUND CUES

Two tape decks are used for this production.
First tape deck has all the sound effects.
Second tape deck has rain and one sound effect.
There will be cues when both tape decks are playing at the same time.
Upstage speaker should be a small phonograph speaker.
Downstage speakers are 2 large boxlike structures hanging from the wings, stage right and stage left.
*Jacksonville 4 (A, B & D) is the taped voice of Sue Belle and Evelina speaking the same lines each time.
†Jacksonville 4 (C) is Evelina's voice only with a space left for Sue Belle to reply to the tape.
Music used in this production, "Honey Love" by Clyde McPhatter and the Drifters, "Blue Moon" by The Marcells.

FURNITURE PROPERTY LIST

KITCHEN:
  kitchen table
  3 kitchen chairs
  1 small table lamp
  shelf stand
  foodstuff on shelves
  hot plate
  sink
  cabinet
  ice box

LIVING ROOM:
  day bed
  large chair
  end chair
  2 foot rugs

BEDROOM:
  bed and mattress
  1 pillow
  1 foot rug
  phonograph (practical)
  dresser
  1 small table lamp
  stack of 45 records
  stool
  vanity
  cardboard closet (practical)

OTHERS:
  palms
  clothesline and laundry
  5 panels
  black velvet portals

COSTUME PROPERTY LIST

SUE BELLE:
Act One:
first light blue slip
light blue cotton underpants
short muslin robe (flowery blue washed out and frayed)
(no shoes)
Act Two:
second light blue slip
red dress (1950's style)
red strap high heels
red earrings
short muslin robe (flowery blue, washed out and frayed)

MAMA:
Act One:
dress with stripes (brown, grey and beige)
brown flat house shoes
orchid robe (faded)
black lace church shoes
wedding ring
cross on chain
brown and white flowery dress
heavy cotton stockings

Act Two:
long beige lace gown
long white church robe with head dress
black lace church shoes
orchid robe (faded)
brown flat house shoes
wedding ring

EVELINA:
Act One:
yellow shorts
pink blouse (midriff)
shoes (brown and white saddle oxfords—dirty)
socks (light purple)
head scarf (yellow)

black half slip
black strapless bra
red strap high heels
hair barrettes
red earrings
red dress (1950's style)
red hand bag
black wig (cut bangs and flip ends)
Act Two:
wears the same things in Act Two

JESUS:

Act One:
long floor length robe (cream color)
shoulder piece hangs over (darker cream)
Jesus sandals
wig, mustache and beard

THE WHITE MAN:

Act Two:
brown suit—(cheap summer weight)
shoes—(brown weaved)
beige shirt
brown socks
tie (brown and white tone)
handkerchief

EDDIE—DADDY:

slacks (color—steel blue)
3 shirts (gold, orchid and beige) used weekly by Actor
sports jacket (brown, wine and grey stripes)
ties (white or hot pink) used weekly by Actor
rain coat (dark brown)
tweed cap
brown socks
sunglasses
handkerchief
thin brown belt
short sleeve undershirts

Act Two:
wears the same things in Act Two

COSTUME PROPERTY LIST

SPECTRES:

Act One and Two:
women dressed in long white robes and white head dresses, black church shoes with felt on soles
men dressed in dark suits with light color shirts and black ties, black shoes with felt on soles
felt is used so there will be no sound when they are on stage

PROPS ON PROP TABLE

2 packs of cigarettes and matches (Winston and Pall Mall)
5 books
    (a) 2 comic books
    (b) 1 drama book
    (c) notebook
    (d) 1 English book
cardboard brown suitcase
brown church hat and handbag
large pair of scissors
sandwich in napkin (half)
Mama's church robe
3 sheets (full bed size)
3 wreaths
1 tamborine

WORKING PROP PLOT

Act One—Preset

On Vanity-Bedroom, Upstage-Upper Level
  pencils
  combs and brushes
  ashtray (on shelf under vanity)
  1 burner hot plate
  1 curling iron
  1 hot iron
  hair greases
  several cheap cosmetics and powder puff and atomizer
  round standing mirror
  long handle mirror
  Evelina and Sue Belle special jewelry (barrettes and earrings)

On Dresser-Bedroom, Upstage-Upper Level
  1 comb and 1 brush
  2 strips of hair ribbon
  stack of 45 RPM records
  small record player (practical)
  2 night gowns (inside 2nd drawer)
  lamp with Jesus statue (removeable)
  several white baby dolls (in stack)

On Bed—Bedroom, Upstage-Upper Level
  bed dressing (sheet, pillow case and bedspread)
  bottle of southern comfort (¾ full, on floor under head of bed)
Special Doll Arrangement on head of bed

In Closet—Bedroom, Upstage-Upper Level
  Evelina's red dress

On Window Sill—Bedroom, Upper Level
  special doll arrangement on window sill

In Kitchen—Downstage Right
  large brown shopping bag (between ice box and sink)
  bottle of milk (inside ice box ½ full)

four glasses (on sink)
ashtray (on sink)
2 burner hot plate (on shelf—this is kit, stove)
dinner pot (on kitchen stove)
lunch box (on ice box with Petal (doll) inside)
long handle spoon (on kitchen stove)
bible (on kitchen table)
small lamp (on kitchen table)
coffee pot (on kitchen stove)
coffee cups (on kitchen table)
half loaf of bread in brown bag (inside ice box)
shelf (food on shelves)

In Livingroom—Downstage Left
small brown shopping bag (place stage left on floor next to wall of stairs)
inside—
   food stuffs
   box of 48 crayons (1 special crayon for drawing)
   sheet of 18 by 24 newsprint (folded)
ashtray—(on end table)
statue of praying hands—(on end table)
worn out picture—(under S. L. end of day bed)

Act Two—Preset

Strike:
comic books and cigarettes from under mattress

Set:
on kitchen table:
half loaf of bread, knife, mustard, package of meat

Reset:
chairs in tight to kitchen table

Reset:
dolls on bed to foot of bed

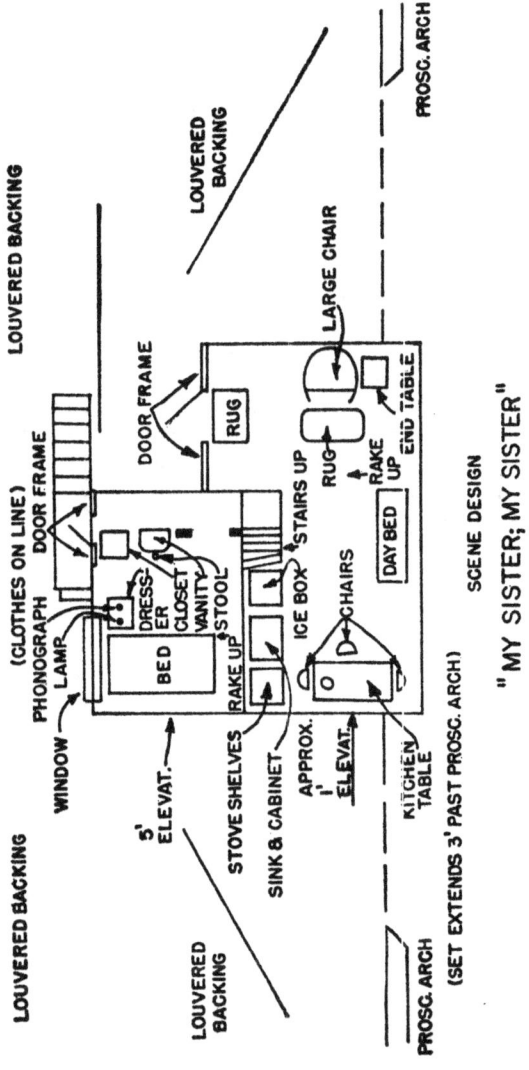

WHITE BUFFALO
Don Zolidis

Drama / 3m, 2f (plus chorus)/ Unit Set

Based on actual events, WHITE BUFFALO tells the story of the miracle birth of a white buffalo calf on a small farm in southern Wisconsin. When Carol Gelling discovers that one of the buffalo on her farm is born white in color, she thinks nothing more of it than a curiosity. Soon, however, she learns that this is the fulfillment of an ancient prophecy believed by the Sioux to bring peace on earth and unity to all mankind. Her little farm is quickly overwhelmed with religious pilgrims, bringing her into contact with a culture and faith that is wholly unfamiliar to her. When a mysterious businessman offers to buy the calf for two million dollars, Carol is thrown into doubt about whether to profit from the religious beliefs of others or to keep true to a spirituality she knows nothing about.

SAMUELFRENCH.COM

SKIN DEEP
Jon Lonoff

Comedy / 2m, 2f / Interior Unit Set

In *Skin Deep*, a large, lovable, lonely-heart, named Maureen Mulligan, gives romance one last shot on a blind-date with sweet awkward Joseph Spinelli; she's learned to pepper her speech with jokes to hide insecurities about her weight and appearance, while he's almost dangerously forthright, saying everything that comes to his mind. They both know they're perfect for each other, and in time they come to admit it.

They were set up on the date by Maureen's sister Sheila and her husband Squire, who are having problems of their own: Sheila undergoes a non-stop series of cosmetic surgeries to hang onto the attractive and much-desired Squire, who may or may not have long ago held designs on Maureen, who introduced him to Sheila. With Maureen particularly vulnerable to both hurting and being hurt, the time is ripe for all these unspoken issues to bubble to the surface.

"Warm-hearted comedy ... the laughter was literally show-stopping. A winning play, with enough good-humored laughs and sentiment to keep you smiling from beginning to end."
- TalkinBroadway.com

"It's a little Paddy Chayefsky, a lot Neil Simon and a quick-witted, intelligent voyage into the not-so-tranquil seas of middle-aged love and dating. The dialogue is crackling and hilarious; the plot simple but well-turned; the characters endearing and quirky; and lurking beneath the merriment is so much heartache that you'll stand up and cheer when the unlikely couple makes it to the inevitable final clinch."
- NYTheatreWorld.Com

SAMUELFRENCH.COM

www.ingramcontent.com/pod-product-compliance
Lightning Source LLC
Chambersburg PA
CBHW070647300426
44111CB00013B/2309